At the Heart of Luke

At the Heart of Luke

Wisdom and Reversal of Fortunes

MARTIN EMMRICH

Foreword by
DAN MCCARTNEY

☙PICKWICK *Publications* • Eugene, Oregon

AT THE HEART OF LUKE
Wisdom and Reversal of Fortunes

Copyright © 2013 Martin Emmrich. All rights reserved. Except for brief quotations in critical publications or reviews, no part of this book may be reproduced in any manner without prior written permission from the publisher. Write: Permissions. Wipf and Stock Publishers, 199 W. 8th Ave., Suite 3, Eugene, OR 97401.

Pickwick Publications
An Imprint of Wipf and Stock Publishers
199 W. 8th Ave., Suite 3
Eugene, OR 97401

www.wipfandstock.com

ISBN 13: 978–1–61097–904–7

Cataloguing-in-Publication Data

Emmrich, Martin

    At the heart of Luke : wisdom and reversal of fortunes / Martin Emmrich.

    xii + 138 p. ; 23 cm. — Includes bibliographical references.

    ISBN 13: 978–1–61097–904–7

    1. Bible. N.T. Luke XIV–XVI—Criticism, interpretation, etc.. 2. Bible N.T. Luke—Parables. I. Title.

BS2595.2 E45 2013

Manufactured in the U.S.A.

"To the man from Nazareth,
the God from Heaven,
who gave us stories."

Contents

Author's Preface · ix
Foreword by Dan McCartney · xi

Introduction · 1

1 A Theological Program for Luke 14–16: Mary's Magnificat · 16
2 The Heart of the Lukan Gospel: Luke 14–16 · 22
3 Exposition · 39
4 Wisdom as Calculation and Humility in Light of God's Activity · 102
5 Reversal and the Lukan *Sondergut* Parables · 111

Conclusion · 124

Bibliography · 131

Author's Preface

THE PRESENT WORK IS the outgrowth of protracted contemplation on the so-called Lukan parables, particularly the four main parables (The Great Banquet, The Lost Sons, The Dishonest Manager, The Rich Man and Lazarus) located in Luke 14–16. The parables of Jesus have always been an object of special interest for me, and Jesus' stories unique to Luke have occupied a prominent place in my personal studies. Over the course of the years of reflecting on the biblical text, the three chapters of Luke 14–16 continued to intrigue me, since the material assembled in them evinces an ostensibly high degree of internal thematic coherence. A good part of this volume, therefore, is concerned with an appreciation of the complex textual unity inherent in this longer section of Luke's gospel. After having identified the theme of reversal of fortunes as the most salient common denominator tying the material together, I concentrated my efforts towards producing a treatise that takes account of my findings. One of the things I soon discovered during my continued studies was that the concept of reversal in Luke 14–16 is to some extent also intertwined with popular Jewish wisdom themes; indeed, that the entire text block takes its cue from a programmatic wisdom saying of reversal (Luke 14:11) that could well appear in a traditional sapiential work like Proverbs. This led to a reading of the text that combines wisdom and reversal themes as the twin unifying factors of the three chapters, a fairly novel approach to the material. The present study does not intend to deny the well documented notion of the presence as well as prominence of the prophetic elements in Luke 14–16 and the gospel as a whole. It attempts to draw attention to a voice in the text that has so far not received much of a hearing, and if the work will therefore spawn reflection and discussion, I shall be satisfied.

Author's Preface

I am indebted to those who have contributed to this volume, especially to Dr. Dan McCartney, Dr. Stephen Baugh, and Dr. Stephen Taylor, as well as others whose reading of the manuscript and subsequent criticism has been much appreciated and helped me to anticipate possible feedback. I am also thankful for the many fine commentaries and monographs (not to speak of numerous articles) on the gospel of Luke, without which a work like this would be rather difficult to conceive. It is my heartfelt wish and prayer that this volume will help Christ's church to gain yet a little more light on the text and the gospel under consideration in order to follow our Lord closely. *Glory to God in the Highest!*

Foreword

Luke's Gospel is the gospel of surprise. Jesus was constantly amazing people both by things he said and things he did, and Luke vividly portrays the paradigm-shifting, world-altering words and deeds of Jesus as divine challenges to "business as usual." The coming of God's reign in the teaching of Jesus means, among other things, a reversal of the world's order of things, such that the important, powerful and wealthy are cast down, and the poor, despised and weak are lifted up. Students of the New Testament frequently refer to this as the "eschatological reversal" because it represents that intrusion of God's restorative justice as the ending of the old age and the inauguration of the promised new age. This reversal is especially prominent in Luke, and even today Luke's stories continue to astonish, especially those parables not found in the other Gospels. Indeed some of these parable are almost mysterious—they leave us scratching our heads.

Dr. Emmrich here shows how the great praise song of Mary in Luke 1 (the "Magnificat") sets the stage for Luke's telling of the story of Jesus as the story of God's great reversal of things. He then focuses on Luke 14–16, chapters which contain material that is almost entirely unique to Luke. Emmrich presents these chapters as the "heart of Luke," providing a coherent centering of this astonishing eschatological reversal, an expression of the astonishing wisdom of Jesus, and a revelation of the astonishing character and concerns of God.

The parables of this section are among the most beloved in Christendom. The characters in these parables are vividly drawn; God's love for the poor portrayed in them is extravagant; their sharp reproaches of the rich are almost shocking; their appeal to the common person is poignant. Yet often the real purpose of these parables in Luke is missed. Familiarity has leached out some of the surprise. On the other hand, our

Foreword

distance from the Jewish world of the first century has made some of these parables almost incomprehensible. Dr. Emmrich helps us recover the surprise where it has waned, and sort out the mystification where we have lost context. The result is a much enriched understanding of what Luke was communicating, and how Jesus was challenging the notions of both his opponents and his disciples.

Precisely because these parables are so beloved, yet also strange and un-nerving, they have generated considerable debate about what they mean. The last, climactic parable in these chapters ("The Rich Man and Lazarus") has even precipitated debate about whether it is really a parable! These parables are certainly among the most difficult, and close examination shows that even the "familiar" parables turn out to be far more complex than is at first apparent. So Dr. Emmrich's sure-footed guide to both their Hellenistic Jewish setting and their surprise element is a welcome contribution to the study of Luke's parables.

Whether or not at the end of the day the reader is convinced that Luke 14–16 is *the* heart of Luke's Gospel, it is undeniable that the material in these chapters gives poignant expression to the heart of Luke the Gospel's author, in both the encouragements of its "reversal" message for the poor and weak, and the warnings of that message for the rich and powerful.

If ever Christians cease to be amazed by Jesus' message they are in danger of becoming sleepy and insouciant. Luke clearly intended to awaken his ancient readers to the wonder of Jesus' story, and to allow the good news of eschatological reversal to stamp the character and message of Jesus indelibly on his readers's lives. Dr. Emmrich facilitates our hearing Luke's heart beat again. May our own hearts echo its rhythm.

Dan McCartney
Redeemer Theological Seminary

Introduction

THE POPULARITY OF JESUS' parables can hardly be overestimated. Even in western non-Christian circles some of his stories continue to linger as part of the inventory of common knowledge, so that parables such as the "Rich Fool," the "Prodigal Son," or the "Good Samaritan" are not unheard-of anecdotes. One could argue that Jesus' most famous parables have been recorded in Luke's gospel, and the above-mentioned three stories are representative of the body of literature. Be that as it may, the parables of Jesus have managed to captivate readers' attention over the centuries, and the present work is devoted to the Lukan parables in particular.

The third gospel features an identifiable body of at least ten parables that are unique to this account of Jesus' life.[1] In recent years, a number of

---

1. Greg Forbes speaks of "at least nine" parables, because the Great Banquet (Luke 14:15–24) is often deemed to be an alternate version of Matthew's Wedding Feast (Matt 22:2–14). Cf. Forbes, *The God of Old*, 16. Although the majority of scholars see both parables as having a common origin in Q, I would agree with a fairly sizeable minority of commentators, who argue that despite resemblances between the two, the Great Banquet constitutes a separate story in its own right. The differences between the parables are certainly as striking as the similarities. So Ellis, *The Gospel of Luke*, 194; Blomberg, *Interpreting the Parables*, 237; Smith, *The Jesus of the Parables*, 120; Morris, *Luke*, 255; Kistemaker, *The Parables of Jesus*, 198; Palmer, "Just Married, Cannot Come," 255. Gerd Petzke is ambivalent regarding the issue, cf. *Das Sondergut des Evangeliums nach Lukas*, 134. Still, it seems best to view the two parables as individual stories featuring the very common parabolic motif of the banquet. This theme looms large not only in Jesus' teachings, but is also a recurring aspect of rabbinic parables. Cf. Young, *The Parables*, 178–82.
   What may or may not constitute a parable is somewhat debatable, since Luke also has shorter teaching units that could be classified as parables. Foremost among them are the Tower Builder and the King at War (Luke 14:28–33). Although Luke actually ranks them as παραβολή, ("parable"), these stories differ from the rest of the Lukan parables due to the absence of the pronounced narrative quality, which characterizes

works concentrating on the parables attested to only in Luke have been published, but only a few of them deal with larger textual complexes. The Prodigal Son as an individual story, sometimes viewed as the quintessential message of Luke's gospel in terms of its literary placement and theological statement,[2] has received the lion's share of monographic attention.[3] The remaining contributions evince a very strong focus on material found in the immediate neighborhood of the stories of Luke 15 (the so-called "Parables of the Lost," including the Prodigal Son), namely parables from chapters 14–16. These narrative parables are identified as the Great Banquet (Luke 14:15–24), the Dishonest Manager (Luke 16:1–13), and the Rich Man and Lazarus (Luke 16:19–31).

The emphasis on parables located in these three chapters should not come as a surprise. Almost half of the Lukan parables are concentrated in Luke 14–16, with the overall actual volume (referring exclusively to story length) approaching 65 percent of the parabolic material unique to Luke. This clustering of parables at the center of the travel narrative (and thus at the heart of Luke's gospel) should naturally give rise to the question as to whether the stories and their connective textual tissue consisting of aphorisms and shorter teaching transitions are somehow related—and if so, in what sense? To my knowledge, however, this inquiry has not been pursued in monographic literature.

The present study is an attempt to remedy the situation. As such, it centers on an exegetical investigation of Luke 14–16, read as a complex literary composition in terms of structure, vocabulary, but most importantly, theological reflection. The work argues that Luke arranged the extended passage to function as an exposition of the two main themes of reversal from Mary's Magnificat (1:46–55, humiliation vs. exaltation; rich being made poor and vice versa). The idea of reversal of fortunes in Luke chapters 14–16 conceived in eschatological terms is categorically communicated via proverbial wisdom (Luke 14:11), and allusions to Old Testament sapiential traditions inform the section at various junctions. Viewed from a greater distance, our text block stands as a single, integer

---

the so-called "*Sondergut* parables."

2. The parable is positioned more or less at the center of the travel narrative (Luke 9:51—19:44), and its concern for repentance, forgiveness, and the reception of outlaws certainly looms large in the work. It has been termed the "gospel within the gospel." Cf. Wenham, *The Parables of Jesus*, 123–25.

3. So in Bailey, *Finding the Lost*; Bahr, *Der Verlorene Sohn*; Aus, *Weihnachtsgeschichte*; Pöhlmann, *Der Verlorene Sohn*.

argument, driven by Jesus' interaction with the Pharisees. It comes to its inevitable denouement in the parable of the Rich Man and Lazarus and its unmistakable focus on the afterlife. The reversal has reached its final stage in heaven and hell, respectively, and the reader is left with the processing of the issue of repentance (Luke 16:30–31).

AUTHENTICITY AND EDITORIAL FRAMEWORK

The history of interpretation in Gospel studies is littered with attempts to reconstruct the texts that may or may not stand behind the texts as they appear in the Synoptics, not to speak of Jesus' original words. Nonetheless, there has been a general consensus emerging in 20th century research that Jesus' teaching ministry centered on the use of parables and that the synoptic parables on the whole represent fair records of these stories.[4] Most scholars are willing to concede that the so-called *criteria of authenticity* (i.e., Jewish-Palestinian background, dissimilarity, multiple attestation, general coherence) affirm the reliability of the tradition.[5]

We may, for instance, refer to comparative studies in rabbinic *meshalim* (parables). Even though rabbinic parables do not become a regular feature in Jewish writings until after 70 c.e., it would be reckless to argue that Jesus invented the teaching method.[6] And while Old Testament parallels are few and far between,[7] there can be no doubt that many of the extant 325 Tannaitic parables have their roots in earlier storytelling methodology at home in the local synagogue.[8] The rabbinic parables and those of Jesus show unmistakable parallels both in terms of terminology and common themes.[9]

Insofar as Jesus' parables are similar to the rabbinic stories, they are rooted in the historical and cultural background of first century Palestine, and it is more than likely that he frequently employed this known form of tutelage. Yet, Jesus' stories are also notably dissimilar to those of

---

4. Cf. Ball, *The Radical Stories of Jesus*, 1–14.
5. Forbes, *The God of Old*, 48.
6. Cf. Young, *Jesus and His Jewish Parables*, 236ff.
7. See Evans, "Parables in Early Judaism," 54–61. After consideration of the evidence, the reader will still have to use a good deal of generosity to see valid OT comparisons. In any case, Evans' count comes to ten texts from the OT which could possibly be placed alongside of Jesus' parables.
8. So Young, *The Parables*, 4–5.
9. Cf. Evans, "Parables in Early Judaism," 71–72.

the rabbis, in that they are generally not exegetical of OT texts and feature a unique convergence of Jewish wisdom and eschatology.[10] The fact that Jesus' use of parables was not exegetical may have been a salient reason why his listeners concluded that "he taught as one who had authority, and not as their scribes" (Matt 7:29). Jesus' parables generally do not cite traditional precedents. These distinguishing characteristics differ from typical Jewish literature of the same genre to such a degree that we may be quite certain the gospel writers preserved authentic Jesus tradition in the parables. The lack of early Christian parallels makes Jesus also stand out among his followers, whose preservation of the otherwise inapposite use of such stories (in early Christian documents besides the gospels) urges the conclusion that they present us with an accurate recollection of Jesus' original proclamation of the kingdom of God.[11]

This affirmation of firm historical footings is applicable to Luke's record of parables unique to his "biography."[12] Although there have been claims of Luke fabricating *Sondergut* parables in accord with his theological agenda,[13] several considerations militate against this approach.

Luke certainly consulted eyewitnesses in producing his gospel (cf. Luke 1:1–4). Their contributions together with the data from written sources (and I assume that such already existed) provide a strong link with the Jesus of history. Yet, the very fact that Luke's classical opening paragraph (1:1–4) mentions the testimony of such eyewitnesses also underscores the author's public accountability in creating his "orderly account" (1:3).[14] Luke places himself under the scrutiny of those who had been "ministers of the word" (1:2) from the very beginning and thus makes himself responsible for the adequate and faithful reproduction of the tradition.

With this claim to historical verity and public accountability Luke denies himself the privilege of a literary *tour de force* by fabricating stories from or about Jesus. Critics were standing by to protest had Luke been found guilty of violating the trust of their input. Given the outstanding

---

10. Cf. Hultgren, *The Parables of Jesus*, 8–10.

11. On the definition and use of the criteria of authenticity, see Blomberg, *Historical Reliability*, 246–54. Stein, "The 'Criteria' for Authenticity," 225–63.

12. Throughout this work I will use the term "biography" in a general sense. I do not intend to imply that the gospel genre is to be viewed in terms of the popular Greek *bioi*.

13. So, for example, in Goulder, *Luke. A New Paradigm*. Vol. 1, 93–107.

14. Bailey draws attention to this idea in *Finding the Lost*, 44.

Introduction

character of the Lukan parables and the considerable "size" of this body of literature, the conjuring up of such material would only invite the prompt rejection of those who knew better. One could, of course, argue that Luke actually *did* commit the dilettantish blunder of placing himself under the judgment of eyewitnesses in order to invite the demolition of his own carefully worded claim to historical reliability. But should we reduce the Lukan parables of Jesus (or Luke's gospel as a whole) to such an unfortunate authorial stumble?

It is clear from a comparison of Matthew and Mark that gospel writers enjoyed a good measure of editorial freedom in composing their versions of Jesus' ministry. In some sense, this freedom had always been characteristic of Jewish Old Testament historiography, so heavily freighted with theological agenda. In regards to our section of the third gospel (14–16), therefore, I affirm Luke's creativity in arranging and shaping the tradition as the eminent theologian that he was, and a variety of relevant details will be discussed in the following chapters of this work. On the other hand, Luke's editorial interventions did not result in a wholesale distortion of Jesus' teachings, nor did he use free composition of stories in pursuit of his own ideology.

This being the case, the present study assumes that Luke 14–16 features early authenticated material that originated with Jesus' teachings. Its selection and arrangement reflects the author's theological rendering of tradition. This unique authorial interest does not coincide with every single word of Jesus on a one-to-one equation, and it may incorporate sayings of Jesus that were voiced on occasions other than indicated in the immediate context.[15] Luke's editorial arrangement and his drawing on the wider pool of authenticated sayings of Jesus serves the purpose of throwing into bold relief certain aspects or implications of Jesus' words and actions as he saw them. The finished work is in a sense as much Luke's own *creative* interpretation of the tradition as it is an adequate reflection of the *ipsissima vox* of Jesus of Nazareth. History and literature are not being polarized in our study of Luke 14–16.[16]

The card of Luke's theological agenda and creativity can, of course, easily be overplayed at the expense of the realization that Jesus himself was a "theologian" and not merely a wandering storyteller. We can be certain that the structure of his discourses and the free adaptation of

---

15. One should keep in mind, too, that the travel narrative (Luke 9:51—19:44) shows a remarkable paucity of chronological and topographical notes.

16. The same is commendable for gospel studies in general.

more or less prominent teachings had the power to create "new" meanings from material already familiar to his disciples. There is no reason to suppose that parables were not also recycled in this way. The challenge of distinguishing such instances from Luke's editorial intervention is very demanding and will always remain somewhat speculative. This is all the more relevant for the Lukan parables, since they have no parallels in the Synoptics. Yet, in the final analysis, Luke wrote the third gospel, not Jesus of Nazareth. This would mean that whether or not Luke preserved larger portions of Luke 14–16 in their original sequence, he made conscious decisions to either preserve or rearrange the material based on his understanding of it. The author's choice and selectivity in turn connects with his theological agenda and purpose for creating the document.

The issue is further complicated by the often-raised question of underlying written sources. I will not test the reader's patience (or mine) in attempting to provide yet another history of investigation in the persistent synoptic problem. There are splendid summaries and introductions that may be consulted.[17] May it suffice to state here that the best we can do is engage the text as it stands in Luke's gospel, realizing that any hypothetical reconstruction of the "original" text or version of a parable can only remove us further from what raises the claim of being historically reliable. [18]

The choice of concentrating our efforts on the present (final) version of the text is also concomitant with the conviction that it is *revelation*. For us who never had the privilege of hearing Jesus' voice, the truth is not to be sought in dubious reconstructions. The text itself is revelation and is intended to be heard as the voice of God.

What is to be interpreted then is not the "original" parable or text but the parable in its canonical context. More than that, while it is appropriate to ask what a parable might have meant in its first century Palestinian setting, the foremost task of the interpreter is not to penetrate the mind of the historical Jesus. Language consists of words, phrases and expressions, not to speak of imagery, pertinent to a particular culture. We are bound to ask questions about what the imagery of the shepherd communicated in Jesus' times, or how Jews thought of Samaritans,

---

17. To name just a few, see Blomberg, *Historical Reliability*; Farmer, *The Synoptic Problem*; McKnight, *Interpreting the Synoptic Gospels*; Stein, *The Synoptic Problem*. Despite its relatively antiquated date, Farmer's monograph continues to be one of the best histories of the problem.

18. Cf. Snider, "Rediscovering the Parables," 61–83.

riches, poverty, and sickness. Knowledge of such matters will inform our understanding of the parables, but it must be remembered that it will always be the synoptic *text* that remains to be interpreted. The canonical text is the product of authorial intention, both human and ultimately divine, and it is in this reality, the text conveying the author's intention, that we seek meaning. Any critical alternative that fails to take account of the transmitted text as the primary object of historical investigation will necessarily (or, *un*necessarily) accumulate speculations and result in little more than a hermeneutical experiment.[19] On the other hand, insofar as the gospels are reliable historical documents, they certainly afford some access into the mind of Jesus of Nazareth. Moreover, the present work presupposes continuity between the mind and intention of the historical Jesus and the mind of the divine author, whose intention comes to expression in the finished text of the NT.

ALLEGORY AND ALLEGORIZING

Our claim to exegetical engagement of the text also brings us face to face with the history of interpretation of Jesus' parables, a topic that will here only be summarized with a few broad strokes.[20]

Adolf Jülicher's (1857–1938) most influential 1888/1899 two-volume monograph[21] signaled a paradigm shift in hermeneutical discussion on the parables. Despite the protest of Luther and Calvin,[22] parables were still considered allegories by most Christian interpreters well into the modern era, with nearly every story detail being pregnant of some doctrinal or historical truth. Jülicher's Aristotelian distinction between *simile* and *metaphor* was the basis for his novel claim that Jesus' parables are to be classified as similitudes. Unlike metaphor and allegory, a similitude is an overt, single-point comparison (*tertium comparationis*) that does not require interpretation. With only one point of contact between image and referent, each parable relates no more than one general truth about the kingdom of God. Jülicher relegated interpretive comments with

---

19. The same concern is expressed in Hultgren, *Parables*, 12–19. See also Gerhardsson, "If We Do Not," 321–35.

20. A fine history can be found in Snodgrass, "From Allegorizing to Allegorizing," 3–29.

21. Jülicher, *Gleichnisreden*.

22. Cf. Kissinger, *The Parables of Jesus*, 44–56.

allegorical features in the Synoptics (cf. Matt 13:49–50; Mark 4:14–20) to the evangelists' creativity and purpose in addressing their respective communities,[23] thus driving a wedge between Jesus and alleged later tradition.

Although Dodd[24] and more recently Jeremias[25] followed Jülicher in his attempt to remove allegory from Jesus' parables,[26] few—if any—contemporary scholars would classify the parables as simile in the above mentioned sense. Blomberg's detailed analysis has made a convincing case that most parables cannot be held to a single point of comparison.[27] The same would be true for rabbinic parables, which share common ground with gospel parables in that they too contain allegorical elements. Like some of Jesus' stories, rabbinic parables often conclude with their respective interpretation featuring multiple points of comparison. There is no reason to suggest that the rabbinic interpretive addenda are not authentic, and the same goes for Jesus' explanations which have often been so easily dismissed as secondary. Where the gospels preserve such appendices, symbolic representation is shown to be more complex than to limit it to one idea. Again, where Jesus' parables do *not* have explanatory conclusions, the interpreter faces the challenge of properly recognizing allegorical elements.[28] However, there should be no *a priori* commitment as to how many comparisons a text may or may not hold.

In any case, Jülicher's hermeneutical approach to the parables did not derive from a focus on their Jewish background but relied on dubious (or rather, artificial) parallels from Greek rhetoric.[29]

The notion of reducing the parables to a single point of comparison and thus the denunciation of allegory may well have been conceived in (over-) reaction to the all too common practice of "allegorizing" in

---

23. Jülicher, *Gleichnisreden*, 1–148.

24. Dodd, *The Parables of the Kingdom*.

25. Jeremias, *The Parables of Jesus*.

26. Snodgrass points out, however, that neither Dodd nor Jeremias managed to be consistent in their approach by reintroducing allegorical elements in their interpretation of individual parables. See "Allegorizing to Allegorizing," 10.

27. Blomberg, *Interpreting the Parables*, 36–69, 171ff.

28. Jülicher's notion of the parables as self-interpreting (i.e., not being in need of interpretation) is curiously illusory. No matter what kind of literature one examines, the reader can never avoid the question, "What does this mean?"

29. Cf. Fiebig, *Die Gleichnisreden Jesu*. For a well-rounded comparative study of Jewish and gospel parables see McArthur and Johnston, *They Also Taught*, 165ff.

interpreting the parables. Allegory is as much a literary genre as it is a mode of reflection.[30] As such it may be present even in what are otherwise non-allegorical literary forms, as well as it can be operative (as a mode of thinking) in the interpreter's mind. Apart from the challenge of properly identifying allegorical elements embedded in a text, the creative engagement of the reader in producing symbolical referents where the author did not intend them appears to be a perennial pitfall.

The tendency of allegorizing the parables has more recently found a contemporary outlet in literary criticism, and more particularly in reader-response hermeneutics. Accordingly, the term "polyvalence" is employed to signify the parables' openness to multiple meanings parented by reading them in non-literary alien contexts.[31] It is certainly valid to argue that the interpretive task is in some sense also an artistic process. But a text's context (here, the parables' canonical context) defines the limits of the reader's creative interaction with the object of investigation. Without this controlling function of the text's own literary world, readers are free to hatch a context of their own making and thus assume the role of the storyteller rather than that of the listener.[32] While such an approach may still be called interpretation, meaning is no longer located in the textual deposit communicated literally but in the reader's mind. It can no longer claim to operate from within the author's world of thought (so far as it is accessible through the text) but instead generates its own parallel universe.

When Jesus spoke in parables, notwithstanding different settings in his ministry that might have modified the meaning of earlier speech acts, he meant to communicate a tangible message. The gospel writers sought to preserve that message within their own theological agenda. Neither Jesus nor the evangelists were conscious of offering "unlimited possibilities" to the interpreter.[33] Therefore, I can appreciate some of the interesting conclusions of the reader-response interpretations, but the more radical the approach is in creating meaning in separation from the textual nexus, it must be seen for what it is, namely, playful interpretive anarchy.[34]

30. Sider argues this point convincingly in *Interpreting the Parables*.

31. So, for example, Tolbert, *Perspectives on the Parables*, 63–93, 102–8; Tolbert, "The Prodigal Son," 1–20; Wittig, "A Theology of Multiple Meanings," 97.

32. Cf. Snodgrass, "From Allegorizing to Allegorizing," 21.

33. Forbes, *God of Old*, 47.

34. See Thiselton, "Reader Responsibility Hermeneutics," 79–113.

In summary, the present analysis proceeds under two fundamental premises. The first is that parables contain allegorical elements with more than one point of comparison (where applicable). Secondly, the literary framework (i.e., canonical context) informs the meaning of the story. In stating the matter this way, we also assume that Luke's authorial intention is accessible to us via textual interaction.

3. WISDOM AND THE LUKAN PARABLES

Wisdom language as well as wisdom concepts figure prominently in Luke 14–16, and, more generally, in the Lukan parables. A few introductory remarks about the situation are in order.

Parables are by definition wisdom discourse.[35] Parables primarily belong in the tool belt of the teacher and the sage, and as such Jesus used them dialogically. This is evident from the fact that many of his parables begin with a question addressing the hearers.[36] The Lukan parables are no different in this regard. Nearly all of them invite dialogue via initial questions,[37] or function as a specific response to some question or behavior on the part of the audience.[38] The stories of Jesus thus assume the interactive life setting of the sage/teacher and the listener, and they aim at character formation. Hendrickx sketches the instructional scenario as follows:

> The parables of Jesus are almost always concerned with the behavior of the listeners: either they deal directly with their behavior or, where this does not seem to be the case and the parable's purport seems rather theological, they are ultimately still concerned with behavior. Even if the listeners must change their point of view, the ultimate intent is a change of behavior in

---

35. See Witherington's considerations on the subject in *Jesus the Sage*, 155–65. Witherington argues that Jesus stylizes himself as a sage of the common people whose parables and aphorisms of counter order challenged traditional Jewish Wisdom concepts.

36. Hendrickx draws attention to this in *The Parables of Jesus*, 3.

37. Cf. "Who among you . . .," 11:5; "Do you think . . .," 13:2, 4; "What man of you . . .," 15:4; "What woman . . .," 15:8.

38. The only exception is Luke 18:1–8 (Persistent Widow). Jesus is said to have told this parable "to the effect that they ought always to pray and not lose heart" (18:1). The parable of the Dishonest Manager (Luke 16:1–9) is introduced with the words, "He also said to his disciples . . ." (16:1), but it is positioned to be an integral part of the larger teaching discourse of Luke 14–16 with its distinctive setting.

consequence of a new outlook on reality. Insofar as the parables teach something, it is always a teaching which should become part of life. It should result in conversion, reconciliation, etc.[39]

Naturally, this mode of discourse suits the role of the sage. Challenging this premise, however, a recent article by Kline Snodgrass maintains that, ". . .parables are the language of prophets. Parables are prophetic instruments."[40] Now, there can be no doubt that Jesus was perceived to be a prophet (cf. Luke 7:16) and that much of what he did had a prophetic ring to it. Nor is it reasonable to suggest that Jesus did not also see *himself* as a prophet (and indeed more than a prophet, cf. Luke 11:32). But to characterize parables as "the language of the prophets" is overstating the case. At best one could argue that "parables seem to have been a modification or extension of wisdom speech first *offered*[41]by prophets."[42] Yet, if "parable" is to refer to a *literary* category (not *acted* parables), and if "parable" denotes a literary *genre*, what do we have? How many OT texts could justifiably be compared to Jesus' parables in both form and content? Using a good deal of generosity, we might well count them on no more than our two hands![43]

The extreme paucity of evidence from the prophets forces the conclusion that parables are not the instrument of the prophet so much as they are the instrument of the sage. As indicated above, there are some 325 Tannaitic parables which are similar to Jesus' stories in terms of form and, to some extent, content. These rabbinic parables may be later than Jesus' parables, but they still show that parables are teaching tools of the sages.[44]

39. Hendrickx, *The Parables of Jesus*, 9
40. Snodgrass, "A Hermeneutics of Hearing," 68–69.
41. Emphasis provided by the author.
42. Cf. Witherington, *Jesus the Sage*, 183.
43. Ten would be Evans's count, see "Parables in Early Judaism," 54–61.
44. Nearly half of the rabbinic parables feature a king, who almost invariably represents God, a feature also known from Jesus' parables. Moreover, the terminology and structure of the rabbinic parables vis-à-vis Jesus' stories compels the conclusion that teaching in parables was a stock trade of the sage. Rabbinic parables will often begin with expressions like: "I will give you a parable. To what does this matter compare? To a man with whom the king deposited an object of value . . ." (*Abot R. Nat.*, version A, ch. 14). Very similar openings are found in Jesus' parables (cf. "With what can we compare the kingdom of God, or what parable shall we use for it? It is like a grain of mustard seed, . . ." Mark 4:30–31; cf. also Luke 13:18). For further discussion on form and content of rabbinic parables see Young, *Jesus and His Jewish Parables*, 236–52.

It is also noteworthy that while parables speak to their audience in a religious context as part of a religious community, they do so in conventional, mostly non-religious terms. They identify religious life with life itself at the most fundamental level.[45] This secularity is a hallmark characteristic of wisdom speech/literature. So parables are sapiential discourse, and in light of the fact that almost one third of Jesus' teachings come in the form of parables, it is fair to say that the parables portray Jesus first and foremost of all as a sage, notwithstanding the presence of most important prophetic themes such as eschatology.[46]

Luke develops the theme of Jesus the ultimate sage in conspicuous ways. At the very beginning of the gospel we read in Luke 2:52: "Jesus increased in wisdom and in stature and in favor with God and man." The language aims at recreating the aura of OT historical narrative, and the informed reader is to recognize the literary echo from 1 Sam 2:26 ("Samuel grew in stature and favor with God and man"). At the very least, therefore, Luke pictures Jesus as a new Samuel, a prophetic leader and judge who possesses God's blessing and communicates it to the people. Luke's episode of Jesus' stay in the Temple further helps to make the connection with Samuel audible, since the prophet too was linked with the sanctuary.[47] We may add to this the fact that Mary's Magnificat (Luke 1:46–55), which looms large in the opening chapters of the third gospel (see below), indulges in reminiscence of Hannah's prayer (1 Sam 2:1–10).

However, the distinct comment from Luke 2:52 carries an additional layer of literary fabric from the OT, namely wisdom literature. Luke's remark about wisdom and favor may as well be seen as having been lifted from Israel's oldest sapiential tradition. Prov 3:1–4 urges the search for wisdom of God, and the net result of the pursuit of wisdom is that "You will find favor . . .in the sight of God and man" (Prov 3:4). Given the overt similarity of language, we may not discount the possibility that Luke in 2:52 also had Proverbs 3 in mind. In other words, he may have blended the two OT traditions (prophetic and sapiential) to form an integrated

---

45. Cf. Hendrickx, *The Parables of Jesus*, 13.

46. That Jesus' parables are pregnant with eschatological references needs no further discussion. See the above comments.

47. In Samuel's case, devotion to the service at the tabernacle was total, in that the sanctuary became his permanent home. Jesus returns to Nazareth and submits to parental authority, but his staying behind in Jerusalem while Joseph and Mary presumed the youngster to be among the traveling company suggests that like Samuel, he was "lent to the LORD" in some special sense (cf. 1 Sam 1:28).

Introduction

whole, tailored for the person of Jesus. I would argue for such a scenario for a couple of additional reasons.

First of all, Luke 2:52 includes the crucial term σοφία (wisdom). It is absent from 1 Sam 2:26, and it certainly heightens the probability of a link with Prov 3:1–4, where the central theme identifies with the search and gain of wisdom. Luke refers to the wisdom of Jesus in a very similar comment in 2:40.[48] The Temple episode is thus framed by two corresponding testimonials about the boy's progress in gaining wisdom, and the importance of the theme in understanding the person of Jesus is made explicit.[49] Luke's portrayal of Jesus' astonishing insight in 2:47 is to be read in the same way. The word σύνεσις denotes penetrating understanding of the relevant issues.[50] The author shows Jesus endowed with wisdom and the fear of the Lord, his perception of God's will rises to an extraordinary measure, and the reaction of his audience is commensurate.

The Temple story is pointing to the theme in a more general sense, too. When Jesus sits in the Temple at Jerusalem, what is he doing? Luke 2:47 states that, ". . .he was sitting among the teachers, listening to them and asking them questions . . ." The text indicates that he wants to learn; he is pursuing wisdom at the feet of the sages. It is perhaps significant that this passage marks the first time that Jesus calls God his Father. This detail goes well with the common wisdom concept of a son learning from his father. When therefore Jesus claims that he must be in the house of his Father (Luke 2:49), we are to recognize that this is the place where instruction is given. The son's getting of wisdom and understanding is precisely the point of the father's instruction to the son in Proverbs 3 and elsewhere in wisdom lore. When Jesus is found sitting in God's house in pursuit of wisdom, he has in some sense come "home."[51]

It is not too far fetched to say that Luke depicts Jesus as the ideal son in search for wisdom, on account of which he is the object of God's special attention and favor. When in Luke 3:22 the Father's love for the

---

48. It may be mentioned that John the Baptist receives only one such notice. Also John is merely growing in spirit (Luke 1:80), whereas Jesus' advance is in wisdom, stature, and favor. Jesus' superiority is underscored. Cf. Bock, *Luke 1:1—9:50*, 274.

49. Marshall discusses the origin of the remark from Luke 2:40. He suggests Sir 51:17, another Jewish sapiential work, as the most likely candidate. Cf. Marshal, *The Gospel of Luke*, 130.

50. Isa 11:2 (LXX) uses this word in describing the superior insight of the Servant of Yahweh.

51. Petzke makes this point in *Das Sondergut*, 61: "V.46 beschreibt . . ., wie sich Jesus im Tempel zu Hause fühlt."

Son is expressed in no uncertain terms, the voice from heaven may be heard in response to his devotion to the pursuit of the fear of the Lord.[52]

However this may be, the notion of Jesus as the model sage, even incarnate wisdom, is found at various junctions in Luke's gospel. To mention the two most obvious texts, Luke 7:35 includes the saying, "wisdom is justified by all her children," and Luke 11:49, "Therefore also the wisdom of God says . . ." These statements almost certainly, at least in some sense, refer to Jesus himself as wisdom personified. The same would be true of Luke 11:31, reminding us that the queen of Sheba came from the utmost parts of the earth to hear Solomon's wisdom, but that a greater one that Solomon was present in Jesus.[53]

But what about the Lukan parables, especially the stories contained in Luke 14–16? Form critics sometimes call the *Sondergut* parables *example stories*, namely, stories that contain no metaphors but illustrate some important truth. We have already discussed the question of allegory and metaphor in relation to Jesus' parables elsewhere (see under 2.), so that it is unnecessary here to argue the incorrectness of this classification when it is freighted with such exclusive connotation. Nonetheless, one thing is certain: The Lukan parables are different from other parables of Jesus, and this is not only because they do not begin with the otherwise popular, "the kingdom of God is like . . ." They bear greater resemblance to real stories or mini dramas, and they develop individual characters to an extent that we do not see in other parables. As such, the stories invite the listener to contemplate and act upon the lessons taught from the behavior of the main characters. In virtually all of the Lukan parables, God's character is on display,[54] but so also some attributes of the disciple of Jesus or the "anti-disciple." In this sense, Luke's *Sondergut* is geared towards informing the behavior of the listener in more *specific* ways than most other parables. These instructions tend to have more of a wisdom character to them.

Hultgren indirectly pays tribute to this in classifying six of Jesus' parables as "parables of wisdom," four of which are Lukan parables. It

---

52. Marshall hints at this idea, *The Gospel of Luke*, 123.

53. For a discussion of these and other relevant passages see Witherington, *Jesus the Sage*, 201–8.

54. Forbes argues this point in *God of Old*, 279ff. Accordingly, God is kind and loving, merciful and compassionate, and yet also the sovereign Judge. These divine character traits are not new with Jesus, but have their root and origin in what the OT says about Yahweh.

is particularly significant for this study that three out of those four wisdom parables are located in the complex of chapters 14–16.[55] Hultgren lists The Tower Builder (Luke 14:28–30), The King Going to War (Luke 14:31–33), and The Unjust Steward (Luke 16:1–8) as parables of wisdom. However, it should be noted that the parable of the Wedding Feast (Luke 14:7–11) forms the head of the discourse as a unit prominently featuring proverbial wisdom (cf. Prov 25:6–7), and that the parable of the Great Banquet (Luke 14:12–24) functions as an exposition of the principle set forth in the preceding pericope. The pivotal importance of Luke 14:7–11 and its sapiential teaching for the entire discourse of chapters 14–16 can easily be overlooked. In any case, wisdom provides a strong undercurrent in Luke 14–16, and corresponding references will be made throughout this study.

In the final analysis, however, wisdom language and concepts are only a vehicle—and by no means the only one—of conveying the ultimate message of the passage, which Luke intended to be an exposition of the themes of reversal featured in Mary's Magnificat (Luke 1:46–55). To this we must now turn our attention.

---

55. Hultgren, *Parables*, 129ff.

1

A Theological Program for Luke 14–16: Mary's Magnificat

Luke has two poetic texts strategically positioned in the opening section of his account. The Magnificat and Zechariah's Benedictus (cf. Luke 1:67) fulfill an important function in the author's objective, as they furnish the theological blueprint of the gospel.[1] By pulling together threads from the subsequent narrative, virtually all the main ideas and concepts of the biography are here anticipated. The songs look forward to what God is about to accomplish for his people in the advent of his Son.[2] At the same time, the language peppers the reader with images from and allusions to the OT.[3] The hymns have the cadence of the Psalms and are replete with terminology designed to deliver the aura of OT canonical literature, notwithstanding verbal parallels to deutero-canonical works, especially the Psalms of Solomon.[4] Inasmuch as the Psalms of Solomon

---

1. Whether these poems were voiced by Mary and Zechariah, or whether Luke composed them for his gospel has no bearing on the present concern. For a discussion on the subject see Bock, *Luke 1:1—9:50*, 142–46, 172–75.

2. This is particularly evident in the Magnificat, where God's initiative is underscored by opening many of the poem's lines with active verbs that take God as subject. Cf. Tannehill, *Luke*, 54.

3. Cf. Green, *Luke*, 101–2.

4. Cf. Bovon, *Das Evangelium nach Lukas*, Vol. 1: *Lk 1,1—9,50*, 82–83. Bovon provides a list of parallels between the Psalms of Solomon (first century BCE) and Mary's

A Theological Program for Luke 14–16: Mary's Magnificat

themselves bank heavily on the use of biblical expressions, though, it is fair to call the finished products collages of OT texts.[5]

While both hymns of praise in a way forestall the conclusion of Luke's account[6] and evince strong covenantal overtones (cf. Luke 1:54–55; Luke 1:68–70, 72–73), Zechariah's Benedictus (and in particular the second half) focuses more specifically on the person and mission of Jesus (cf. Luke 1:76–79). The Magnificat, on the other hand, aims at praising God for his acts on behalf of his people. His saving acts are conceived in personal terms, that is, Mary seeing herself as the object of God's mercy (Luke 1:47–49), as well as in more general terms (Luke 1:50–53). The song has thus three parts, with Luke 1:54–55 placing the foregoing thoughts in a covenantal context by highlighting God's faithfulness to his scriptural promises.[7]

The song's language differs from Zechariah's praise in that the latter text (Luke 1:67–80) construes salvation for the people of God in terms of deliverance from enemies (Luke 1:71, 74), whereas the Magnificat speaks of salvation more specifically as reversals of fortunes. Reversal is also couched in more sociological vocabulary,[8] and these general statements about God's salvific intervention are singularly important for setting the theological tone of the third gospel. Tannehill sees the song as an operatic assessment of the entire narrative about to unfold.[9] The action stops, and the reader is given both a summary view and a prospect of God's program for redemption.

The theme of reversal as portraying God's salvific work is conspicuously present in the first two parts of the poem. Mary calls herself a "humble" person (Luke 1:48a), but now God has so favored her that all will call her blessed (Luke 1:48b). The second half, more generally concerned with "those who fear him" (Luke 1:50), is of particular interest

Magnificat.

5. So Green, *Luke*, 101.

6. Note that the closing words of the gospel show the disciples engaged in praising the Lord. Most specifically, Zechariah's pronouncement of blessedness ("Blessed be the Lord God of Israel," Luke 1:68) is echoed in Luke 24:52–53 with the use of very similar vocabulary: "And they worshiped . . . and returned to Jerusalem with great joy, and were continually in the temple blessing God."

7. For a more detailed discussion of the literary unity of the poem see Tannehill, "Magnificat," 263–75; Dupont, "Le Magnificat," 321–43.

8. It should be noted, though, that the "arm of the Lord" (cf. Luke 1:51) is also a war image. See below.

9. Tannehill, *The Narrative Unity of Luke-Acts*, 31.

for our purposes. Here, reversal is communicated on two levels: Those who exalt themselves are being humbled, whereas the humble are exalted (Luke 1:51–52). Again, the rich are dispossessed, while the poor are filled with good things (Luke 1:53).

These two motifs of transposition picture God in twin roles. First, he is the divine warrior accomplishing deliverance for his oppressed people. God shows "strength with his arm" (Luke 1:51) by scattering the proud and exalting those of humble estate (Luke 1:51–52). By the same token, God is the faithful guardian of the covenant, showing favor to the underprivileged and poor of the people, while resisting the proud rich (Luke 1:53). God's care for the marginalized is perhaps the most dominant theme in the travel narrative (Luke 9:51—19:44), the central section of the gospel of Luke.[10] Both images of God as Deliverer reach all the way back to the Mosaic tradition. The "strength" of God's arm is a prominent idiom in the exodus narrative (cf. Exod 6:6; Exod 15:16; cf. also Deut 4:34), and God's concern for the poor and underprivileged is firmly anchored in the Mosaic code (cf. Exod 23:6, 11; Lev 23:22; Deut 15:7–9). At the same time, the socio-economic reversal of Luke 1:53 has close parallels in the Psalter (Ps 107:9; Ps 34:11).[11]

Ringe's comment on the reversal does not go far enough. She claims that, " . . . an economy marked by scarcity and competition is replaced by an economy of generosity in which all have enough: Those who are hungry get to enjoy good things, and those who are rich do not get to add to their riches. The powerful no longer get to exercise power over others, but nothing is said about the 'lowly' now getting to do what has been done to them."[12] While I would have no quarrel with the latter half of the statement, judgment on the formerly powerful and privileged is implicit. In particular, the expression "showing strength with his arm," coupled with the verb "to scatter" indicates that the reversal will ultimately not be brought about by common consent or persuasion, but by a sovereign act of divine judgment. The language is highly reminiscent of the exodus tradition and the demolition of Egyptian power (cf. Ps 89:10; Ps 118:15).[13]

10. Cf. Forbes, *God of Old*, 109.

11. Cf. Ringgren's discussion of the Magnificat's OT background, Ringgren, "Luke's Use of the Old Testament," 230–31.

12. Ringe, *Luke*, 35.

13. Ps 89:10 (LXX) almost certainly provided the *Vorlage* for the line in Luke 1:51. The psalm here reflects on the power of God's arm (βραχίων) and the fate of the arrogant (ὑπερηφάνοι) by using the same vocabulary as Luke 1:51. Even the main verb

A Theological Program for Luke 14–16: Mary's Magnificat

As mentioned above, both of these motifs of transposition have a most copious OT background (cf. Exod 15:3; Exod 22:22–24; Exod 23:6; Ps 24:7–10; Prov 3:34; Isa 42:13; Zech 7:10), but it bears repetition that Mary's song voices key themes that will recur throughout the gospel.[14] As such, the Magnificat is as theological as it is eschatological in thrust. The deliverance contemplated is, after all, the fulfillment of the OT promises and the hopes of God's people.[15]

A few examples from the opening chapters of Luke's gospel keenly demonstrate the centrality of reversal language. Jesus' announcement of the "favorable year of the Lord" in the synagogue of Nazareth (Luke 4:16–21) carries the promise of a reversal of conditions. The poor and oppressed being "set at liberty" (Luke 4:18), the jubilary theology of the OT (cf. Lev 25:8–17; Isa 61:1–2) is here given an eschatological messianic fulfillment in the ministry of Jesus. The normative import of the sermon in Nazareth for the third gospel is beyond dispute.[16]

Dramatic eschatological reversal of fortunes is also the subject of the first longer teaching unit in the gospel. The Lukan Beatitudes (Luke 6:20–23) address poverty and reveal a sense of the miseries of an oppressed class (i.e., the disciples) who are now promised a kingdom and satisfaction. The following Woes (Luke 6:24–26) complete the reversal with a negative contrast. In particular the key words "rich," "full" (πίμπλημι, Luke 6:25), and "hunger" (πεινάω, Luke 6:25) deliver an unmistakable link to the vocabulary of the Magnificat (Luke 1:52–53).[17]

It is the contention of this study that the themes of reversal are of cardinal interest not only for the gospel as a whole, but specifically for Luke 14–16, and a very brief preview of this text block will demonstrate this. Virtually all the material here focuses on the said aspects of reversal.[18] It is quite conspicuous that the first theme of reversal expressed in

---

(διασκορπίζω, "to scatter") has been lifted from Ps 89:10. Since the imagery of the psalmist describes violent intervention against God's enemies, the notion should not be lost in the Magnificat.

14. Cf. Green, *Luke*, 102; Tannehill, *Luke*, 57. The same can be said with respect to the book of Acts, though this is not a concern for the present work.

15. Nolland classifies the hymn "as celebration of eschatological fulfillment." Cf. Nolland, *Luke 1—9:20*, 64.

16. Cf. Sloan, *The Favorable Year*, 1.

17. Sloan believes that the language of the Beatitudes has jubilary overtones and connects it with Luke 4:16–30. While his suggestion has merit, the verbal link with the Magnificat is even stronger. Cf. Sloan, *The Favorable Year*, 123–28.

18. This notion will be discussed in detail in chapters 2 and 3.

the song in Luke 1:51 (the exalted ones being humbled, the humble being exalted) is under consideration in Luke 14:11 at the very beginning of this discourse. The principle is cast in wisdom language, and its wording clearly echoes the dictum of the Magnificat: "Everyone who exalts himself will be humbled, and he who humbles himself will be exalted" (Luke 14:11; cf. also Luke 16:15b).

To this we may add the fact that the second reversal described in Luke 1:53 (the rich being dispossessed, the poor being filled with good things) has a very palpable echo in the conclusion of the teachings of chapters 14–16 in the parables of the Rich Man and Lazarus. Specific literary features help to cement this assertion. Not only *does* the famous parable tell the story of the rich and poor and the reversal of their fortunes, but it too has the memorable language of receiving "good things" (Luke 16:25; cf. Luke 1:53a). Perhaps even the reference to "father Abraham" in the very last line of the Magnificat (cf. also Luke 1:73) affords a parallel to the Rich Man and Lazarus. The rich man twice calls upon "father Abraham" in his address from Hades (Luke 16:24, 30), thus possibly conjoining the complex of parables and teachings with Mary's song.[19] Both ideas of reversal from Luke 1:51–53, therefore, are overtly represented at the beginning as well as the ending of chapters 14–16.

The theme of reversal is also central to the remaining stories and instructional material of Luke 14–16. Luke 14:7–11 speaks for itself, in that this unit has transposition as its central theme and clinches the point with the maxim of Luke 14:11. The parable of the Great Banquet (Luke 14:12–24) expands on the principle of inversion from the preceding pericope: The noble guests who were originally invited are rejected, whereas the mob and the outcasts are being given a reception by the host of the occasion. The principle of reversal with a socio-economic nuance is unmistakable.

The parables of the Lost (Luke 15:1–32) may at first sight have less to do with reversal of fortune. However, the thought lies just beneath the

---

19. It may be mentioned that there are only two instances in Luke's gospel were we hear explicitly of God knowing and judging the hearts of people. One is found in Luke 1:51; the other occurs in Luke 16:15. This may be coincidental, but the context of Jesus' saying in Luke 16:15 provides a strong thematic nexus with the Magnificat. Jesus' point is that God frustrates the hidden attempts at self-justification and self-exaltation of the arrogant, which chimes well with the thought of Luke 1:51 (God scattering the proud in the thoughts of their hearts). Moreover, Luke 16:15b restates the reversal principle known from both the Magnificat and Luke 14:11 ("For what is exalted among men is an abomination in the sight of God").

A Theological Program for Luke 14–16: Mary's Magnificat

surface of the story of the two sons, and it rises to the fore in the father's final remark: " . . . this your brother was dead, and is alive; he was lost, and is found" (Luke 15:32). This statement, in turn, has an anaphoric effect on the parables of the sheep and the coin, respectively, which can now be read through the lens of this sentiment.[20] Luke 15 continues the theme of God's concern for the marginalized and the despised.

The parable of the Dishonest Manager (Luke 16:1–8) deals with the shrewd response of the steward who faces calamity. He does what he needs to do to avoid what seems to be inevitable economic disaster for himself. Even though the reversal never comes full turn or is not fully realized, it is nevertheless implicit: If the manager had indeed lost his position, then poverty and privation would be expected in the thin air of first century Palestine's highly stratified economic system.

As for the Rich Man and Lazarus (Luke 16:19–31), there is no need to point out that reversal of fortune lies at the heart of the parable's message. The case is categorically stated in Abraham's reply to the rich man (Luke 16:25).

A cursory reading of Luke 14–16 reveals how central the idea of inversion is to the main parables of the textual complex. Both the opening and closing pericopes (Luke 14:7–11; Luke 16:9–31) connect with the two themes of inversion from Mary's Magnificat in especially overt ways. The didactic material that connects the parables, and thus helps to create a more or less integer unit, can be shown to function in support of the theme of reversal.[21] The twin theme of reversal from the Magnificat has been deepened and interpreted from diverse angles via the parables and teachings featured in Luke 14–16. Our text can therefore be viewed as an exposition of Mary's song and its central notion of transposition.

Having said all this, it is now time to turn our attention to the text in more detail. In doing so, we will initially focus on the limits of the text and its position in the third gospel, in order to discuss both structure and internal coherence of chapters 14–16. Eventually, textual exposition will furnish the reader with an in-depth analysis of our passage.

---

20. See below the discussion of Luke 15.
21. See the discussion in subsequent chapters.

2

The Heart of the Lukan Gospel: Luke 14–16

CHAPTERS 14–16 ARE FOUND in the central section of Luke's work, the so-called travel narrative (Luke 9:51—19:44). All of the parables unique to Luke's gospel occur within this core section of the work. Forbes argues that "here Luke presents Jesus as the prophet like Moses, on a journey to Jerusalem to effect a new exodus for the people of God."[1] In light of Luke's conscious casting of the travel narrative, he further claims that it is only "appropriate"[2] that the parables, which in his view reveal the character of the God of the exodus, are located in this segment of the gospel.

The material in Luke 9:51—19:44 is unique in several other regards, too. First of all, Egelkraut's redaction critical study has drawn attention to the near absence of chronological or topographical detail.[3] Not only does Luke abandon the Markan sequence of events and teachings until the last of the parables has been included (The Pharisee and the Tax Collector, Luke 18:9–14), but he also uses an unusual amount of material not paralleled in Mark.[4] While Luke records only a few miracles (Luke 13:10-17;

---

1. Forbes, *God of Old*, 329. For a specific example of Luke's presentation of the Jesus tradition in terms of the eschatological exodus see Emmrich, "The Lukan Account," 267–79.

2. Forbes, *God of Old*, 329.

3. Egelkraut, *Jesus' Mission to Jerusalem, Lk 9:51—19:44*, 16–24.

4. The calculation of this section in terms of material unique to Luke has been the

The Heart of the Lukan Gospel: Luke 14–16

Luke 14:1–6; Luke 17:11–19; Luke 18:35–43),[5] teaching discourses, and in particular the Lukan parables, govern this portion of the gospel.

Jesus' audiences in Luke 9:51—19:44 generally alternate between the disciples and his opponents, most notably the Pharisees, and much of the presentation has a polemic edge to it. Bock notes that "up through the end of Luke 14 there is interplay between instruction of the disciples and rebuke of the Jewish leadership."[6] This claim would be in need of some modification. Upon closer examination, Luke 9:51—13:35 shows Jesus facing antagonism from a wide range of groups or individuals. From the Samaritans (Luke 9:51–56), the Galilean cities of Chorazin, Bethsaida, and Capernaum (Luke 10:13–16), a certain lawyer (Luke 10:25–37), Pharisees and lawyers (Luke 11:37—12:3), "someone in the crowd" (Luke 12:13–21), the crowds (Luke 12:54–59), the ruler of the synagogue and "all his adversaries" (Luke 13:17), to the Pharisees and the inhabitants of Jerusalem (Luke 13:31–35), Luke manages to include a great variety of conflicts with no exclusive group being the target of Jesus' rebukes.

It is noteworthy that Luke even leaves Jesus' opponents in the Beelzebul controversy unidentified, opting for the expression "some of the people" in describing the antagonists. Given the popularity of the episode, evident in that all three Synoptic accounts feature the controversy, Luke seems to ignore Matthew's and Mark's identification of the culprits as the Pharisees and scribes, respectively (Matt 12:24; Mark 3:22).[7]

The scenario changes, however, in Luke 14–16. This block of material evinces an unmistakably exclusive focus on the Pharisees, lawyers, and scribes as the active opposition. The text begins by introducing a new setting (Luke 14:1) in the house of a ruler of the Pharisees and sustains the emphasis on the ruling religious class (cf. "the lawyers and Pharisees,"

---

subject of debate, ranging from Egelkraut's more than one-third (*Jesus' Mission*, 27) to about 10 percent. Cf. Resseguie, "Interpretation," 3–36. Bock (*Luke 9:51—24:53*, 959) holds that Resseguie's numbers "are closer to the real percentages, since Luke 9:51—18:14 lacks any significant Marcan parallels."

5. By comparison, Luke 4:14—9:50, the much shorter section of the Galilean ministry, features a total of thirteen miracles.

6. Bock, *Luke 9:51—24:53*, 960.

7. Matt 12:24 and Mark 3:22 are more specific in naming the opposition as the Pharisees (Matthew) and the scribes (Mark). The discrepancy is probably due to the fact that neither evangelist decided to focus on one of the groups that are often shown to act in tandem (cf. Matt 12:38; Matt 15:1; Mark 2:16; Mark 7:1). This being the case, the antagonists in the Beelzebul controversy might have included both scribes and Pharisees.

Luke 14:3; "the Pharisees and scribes," Luke 15:2; "the Pharisees," Luke 16:14) through the end of chapter 16. The alternating pattern of instruction (i.e., Jesus addressing his opponents and his disciples by turns) is particularly consistent in these three chapters,[8] and the conflict between Jesus and the religious rulers builds momentum to reach its climax in the parable of the Rich Man and Lazarus.[9]

Thus, it is in Luke 14–16 that Jesus' way is most emphatically expounded as being at odds with the Jewish religious leadership, which prepares the reader for Jesus' betrayal and passion. At the same time, the conspicuously dense clustering of Lukan parables and sayings also performs the task of positively revealing the character of God and charting the course for Jesus' disciples. The message of Luke's gospel is sharply defined in these chapters, and it is fair to refer to this textual complex as the heart of the Lukan gospel,[10] not the least because Luke 14–16 can be read, as has been intimated in the previous chapter of this study (and will be argued hereafter), as an exposition of the main theological themes of the Magnificat.

Before we can proceed, though, the textual limits of the complex need to be defined more closely.

DEFINING THE LIMITS: LUKE 14:1—16:31

The opening words of Luke 14:1 clearly mark the beginning of a new episode with the Greek Septuagintal formula so typical for the third gospel (καὶ ἐγένετο + ἐν τῷ + infinitive).[11] The chronological reference to the Sabbath enhances the effect of signaling a new occasion.

Scholars have often noted the thematically homogenous character of Luke 14:1–24.[12] All the sub-units of chapter 14 have to do with dinners, hosts, guests, etiquette and behavioral patterns pertaining to such societies.[13] The unitary character of Luke 14 will be subject to investi-

---

8. See the discussion below.

9. Again, see the discussion below.

10. Forbes (*God of Old*, 109) notes that chapter 15 in its literary setting has "rightly been described as the heart of the Third Gospel." However, it is precisely on account of its literary setting, namely, the textual cohesiveness of Luke 14–16 that the adjacent chapters should be included to form the "heart" of the gospel.

11. The formula almost invariably introduces a new episode (cf. Luke 5:12, 17; Luke 6:1, 6; Luke 9:18, 51; Luke 11:1, 27).

12. Cf. Braun, *Feasting*, 15.

13. Luke 14:1–6, the introductory pericope, sets the stage for teachings on table

The Heart of the Lukan Gospel: Luke 14–16

gation in the exposition part of this study.¹⁴ For the time being, we are mainly interested in demonstrating how the opening verses of chapter 14 provide a bridge to chapter 16 via both lexical links and thematic cohesion. The author has arranged Luke 14–16 to form a textual edifice with a remarkably high level of integrity, featuring a beginning and a palpable conclusion to the unit.

Before we further engage the text, though, a disclaimer is in order. I do not intend to raise the false notion that some of the following textual and thematic aspects are unique to Luke 14–16. Indeed, it would be strange if they were to be found only in this section of the gospel, given their importance for the work as a whole. Rather, it is the *concentration* of certain ideas with corresponding features that warrants the conclusion that Luke 14–16 forms a textual complex.¹⁵

Questions About the Law (Luke 14:1–6; Luke 16:16–18)

Luke 14:1–6 hinges on Jesus' question of what the Law teaches: "Is it lawful to heal on the Sabbath, or not?" (Luke 14:3). The lawyers and Pharisees (Luke 14:3) would have answered with a categorical "No!" According to rabbinic regulations, healing miracles (or more generally, healing) on the Sabbath could only be performed if there was an identifiable danger to life.¹⁶ Jesus certainly knew that such was not the case with the man suffering from water retention (dropsy), and so his reference to "lawfulness" must refer to the Mosaic Law. The rabbinic prescriptions in this case were narrower than what the Law demanded, and their rigorous application did in fact communicate a certain absurd indifference to human suffering.

This notion affords a conspicuous parallel to Luke 16:16–18, where criticism of the rabbinic tradition also resonates in Jesus' words. Not only

---

fellowship. It is somewhat different from the following material with its Sabbath-related controversy but, as will be shown below, this focus connects with the conclusion of our text block (Luke 16:14–31).

14. Cf. chapter 3.

15. Additionally, in the ensuing discussion the reader should keep in mind that while any individual point of comparison may be debatable, the argument rests on the *combined* force of the evidence. In light of the sheer number of connections, Luke's intention of arranging the material in such a way as to create an *inclusion* appears more than likely.

16. Cf. Morris, *Luke*, 252. The Mishnah (*m. Sab.* 7.2) had "forty save one" (thirty-nine) prohibitions as to what was unlawful to do on the Sabbath rest.

25

is the subject of his concern expressed as the "Law and the Prophets" (Luke 16:16), but his observations about marriage and divorce (Luke 16:18) show the received tradition to be off the mark once again: Instead of defining the case in even more narrow terms than the Law—as was the case with regard to healing on the Sabbath—some secondary sources on divorce far exceeded the allowance of the Law. At least the Pharisaical school of Hillel found divorce permissible for as little cause as not being able to cook (cf. *m. Git.* 9.10)![17]

Thus, in two incidents located at the beginning and ending of Luke 14–16, Jesus takes aim at Jewish tradition at odds with Moses' Law by either being too restrictive or too freehanded in interpreting Scripture.[18] To this we may add the fact that the parable of the Rich Man and Lazarus (Luke 16:19–31) expresses the concern of attentively listening to "Moses and the Prophets" (Luke 16:29, 31), which idea connects both with the pericope that introduces the parable (Luke 16:14–18), as well as with Luke 14:1–6 and the question of "lawfulness." Hence, this theme can be shown to bracket the discourse of Luke 14–16.

Lexical features deliver additional marks of cohesion and help to strengthen the textual nexus. Luke 14:5 and Luke 16:17 use forms of the verb "to fall" (πίπτω) built on the simple stem πεσ-. Both episodes also employ forms of the verb "to dismiss/pass away" (ἀπολύω, Luke 14:4; Luke 16:18 [2x]).

Honor and Shame (Luke 14:7–14; Luke 16:19–31)

Another notable conjunction between chapters 14 and 16 exists in the salient theme of honor and shame thrown into relief by scenes of table fellowship. The contrast of honor and shame is stated categorically in Luke 14:8–9. Those who seek to honor themselves by choosing the preferred seating experience demotion and shame ("the lowest place," Luke 14:9b). Conversely, those who sit in the lowest place are being promoted to the place of honor (Luke 14:10). This movement is reflected in the parable of the Rich Man and Lazarus.[19] The beggar lives in the misery of social

---

17. The school of Shammai held that immorality was the only ground for divorce and entertained a well-known debate with the school of Hillel. It appears that the Qumran community sided with Shammai's position (cf. 11QTemple 57:11–19).

18. Perhaps it would be even more accurate to speak of the two pericopes that introduce the first and the last of the parables in Luke 14–16, respectively.

19. Ratzinger sees the reversal inherent to the plot of the parable as mirroring a

The Heart of the Lukan Gospel: Luke 14–16

disintegration and the worst physical deprivation (Luke 16:20-21).[20] Yet, upon his death, the pariah finds himself sitting at Abraham's side (Luke 16:22) at the heavenly banquet. This honorific promotion would have been the professed *non plus ultra* of every religious Jew in Israel. As for the rich man, Luke 16:28 tells us that he is being demoted from his perpetual banquet to occupy a "place of torment." The use of the word τόπος ("place," Luke 16:28) echoes the term's four occurrences in Luke 14:8-10 ("place of honor"/"lowest place"). The reversal of honor and shame (promotion and demotion) against the backdrop of banqueting affords a strong link between chapters 14 and 16.

Additional textual features deserve mentioning at this junction. First of all, the exclamation of one of the dinner guests in Luke 14:15 ("Blessed is everyone who will eat bread in the kingdom of God!") does not only occasion Jesus' parable of the Great Banquet (Luke 14:16-24), but notably anticipates Lazarus' advancement by the angels to the heavenly banquet (Luke 16:22). Secondly, the parable of the Great Banquet itself can be seen to forestall the reversal in the Rich Man and Lazarus. The master's ominous verdict on those who had snubbed him (Luke 14:24) carries with it the same kind of finality that characterizes Abraham's words to the rich man in Hades (Luke 16:26), not to speak of the simultaneous promotion of the social outcasts.[21]

Clash of Social Extremes (Luke 14:1-14; Luke 16:19-31)

A number of details surrounding the cast of characters in both Luke 16:19-31 and Luke 14:1-14 further cement the notion of deliberate arrangement by Luke so as to create a definable text unit.[22] We note first of all that Lazarus' designation as a "poor man" (πτωχός, Luke 16:20) corresponds with Jesus' recommendation in Luke 14:13, namely, to "invite the poor" (πτωχός), something that the rich man in the parable refuses to do. The master of the house in the parable of the Great Banquet, however, does better. His charge to his servants is to go to "the streets and lanes of the city, and bring

---

series of Psalms, most notably Ps 44:15-23; 73:3ff. Cf. Ratzinger, *Jesus of Nazareth*, 212-14.

20. Cf. Eckey, *Das Lukasevangelium*, 11:1—24:53, 722-23.

21. See the discussion below.

22. The following observations are intimately related to the previous discussion on honor and shame.

in the poor and crippled and blind and lame" (Luke 14:21). These urban poor would have to be grouped with Lazarus as the perceived "filth" of the city, who relied on handouts in public places and hunting for scraps and leftovers where food was consumed.[23] One can almost see the beggar of the parable in Luke 16 in the master's order to his servants.

But Lazarus' poor physical condition also puts him in the same rubric with the man suffering from water retention (Luke 14:1–6). The latter symptom was often viewed as a divine judgment for sin or uncleanness.[24] Lazarus' profuse skin sores certainly rendered him unpleasant to look upon as well as ritually unclean. Both persons came from the outer social fringe and were in need of mercy. More so, both are in close proximity to the "table" of an eminent individual.[25] Even though Lazarus is only laid at the rich man's gate (Luke 16:20), his desire to be fed with the rich man's crumbs brings his table (τράπεζα, Luke 16:21) into focus. Thus, just as the ἔμπροσθεν ("before," Luke 14:2) communicates the idea that Jesus could not help but see the man,[26] so Lazarus was a constant presence posing a challenge to the rich man's complacency in the parable.[27]

Lazarus' abject condition and craving for the scraps of the rich man's table is portentous of the latter's fate. He will find himself in horrific circumstances hoping for a drop of water from Lazarus to cool his tongue (Luke 16:24). Just as there were no scraps for the beggar, there will be no water for the rich man. On account of the obvious mirroring of images described in the profound inversion, we may suggest that Lazarus also functions as a reminder or warning about the rich man's spiritual condition and expectation from God. His inhospitable agenda and refusal to

---

23. Cf. Braun, *Feasting*, 86–87. Cf. also Esler's depiction of urban poverty in *Community and Gospel*, 179.

24. Cf. Bock, *Luke 9:51—24:53*, 1256. See also Van Der Loos, *The Miracles of Jesus*, 504–6; Strack and Billerbeck, *Kommentar zom Neuen Testament*, 203ff.

25. Braun (*Feasting*, 31) notes that "the social fringe type loitering near elite banquets undoubtedly is to be part of the visualized scene in Luke 14 . . ." Dinners such as the one described in Luke 14:1–6 were often a more or less public affair. Uninvited "guests" were tolerated to stand by and watch the distinguished society. It is therefore not necessary to suppose that the dropsical man was a plant to begin with. He could as well have been there already in order to become the object of the Pharisees' attention. Luke does not bother to clarify the matter, and it is irrelevant to the story. Cf. Blomberg, *Contagious Holiness*, 144–45.

26. Cf. Marshall, *The Gospel of Luke*, 579.

27. The way the parable frames the rich man's words from Hades indicates that he even knew the beggar's name (cf. Luke 16:24).

listen to "Moses and the Prophets" (Cf. Luke 16:29) made him poor and despicable in God's sight (cf. Luke 16:15b), even though it is only after the reversal that this becomes evident.[28]

If this is correct, the dropsical man from Luke 14:1–6 may be seen to perform an analogous function in the episode. Braun advances the intriguing thesis that the man is not merely an uninvited bystander, but a literary figure whose role is to visually represent the host's and his guest's self-indulgent agenda.[29] At least with regard to their desire for being recognized by peers, Luke 14:7 uncovers their inordinateness, an attitude that goes tandem with the ethos of exclusive social interaction. The disposition of wealth or avarice in the more narrow sense of the word will be the charge against the Pharisees in Luke 16:14.[30] Braun may be pushing the envelope in comparing the scene in Luke 14:1–6 to the extravagant Greco-Roman *symposia*, where participants practiced excess to the limit,[31] but could have a point in suggesting that the condition of the dropsical man at the Pharisaic banquet functioned as an ironic clue to the moral character of the religious people at dinner.[32] If so, his presence introduced a vatic element, which may intimate a link with the parable of the Rich Man and Lazarus, where their respective situation in life bespeaks their spiritual state of affairs and expectation for the future (Luke 16:25).

Miracles Failing to Reform Hardened Hearts (Luke 14:1–6; Luke 16:27–31)

Another thematic detail that helps to connect Luke 14 and 16 and so brings closure to the unit is that of miracles failing to create repentance

---

28. Although listening to "Moses and the Prophets" identifies the (still possible) salvation of the rich man's brothers, it is clear that his own failure to "hear them" (Luke 16:29) is what brought him to Hades.

29. Cf. Braun, *Feasting*, 30–42. Braun offers several intertestamental sources for his case. Dropsy was viewed as a punishment for immoral desires. Ironically, dropsy identifies bloating due to water retention (whatever the medical cause) accompanied with an unusual craving for drink. The craving thus serves to feed the disease.

30. A popular comparison among Cynics was to see dropsy as a picture of the vice of avarice. Cf. Braun, *Feasting*, 33.

31. Bloomberg (*Contagious Holiness*, 145) makes a convincing case that Jesus' table fellowship in Luke 14:1–6 (and elsewhere in Luke, cf. *Contagious*, 160–63) did not take the form of Greco-Roman *symposia*. Even if it did, Jesus turned it into the opposite (Luke 14:1–24).

32. Braun, *Feasting*, 40–41.

in those who need it most. Luke 14:1–6 reports a healing miracle leaving the witnesses rather unimpressed with Jesus. Similarly the closing words of the parable of the Rich Man and Lazarus entertain the possibility of "raising someone from the dead." This thought, however, is quickly abandoned on account of the unresponsiveness of the rich man's brothers. A miracle would not change their hearts, since words that someone from the dead could bring them would be no clearer than the Law's teaching of how one ought to treat the poor (cf. Deut 14:28–29; Deut 15:1–3; Deut 23:19; etc.). The implication is that they had already hardened themselves against the voice of God (cf. Luke 7:29–30).[33]

The silence of the Pharisees after Jesus' rebuke and healing of the dropsical man (Luke 14:6), far from being a sign of remorse, is indicative only of their inability to find an appropriate response to the logic of the *a fortiori* argument (cf. Luke 14:5). Despite having witnessed a healing miracle that portrayed the in-breaking of the life and kingdom of God, they remained blind to what God was doing in their midst.

The episode of Luke 6:6–11 is roughly parallel to Luke 14:1–6. It describes a healing miracle on a Sabbath, with the scribes and Pharisees looking on. Their reaction here is described in terms of being "filled with fury" (Luke 6:11). Although Luke 14:1–6 is less explicit in commenting on the Pharisees' state of mind, except that they too were trying to find a reason to accuse Jesus, we may safely assume that the miracle did not "speak" to their hearts.[34] The parable of Luke 16:19–31, aimed at the same group of people (i.e., the Pharisees, cf. Luke 16:14), anticipates the same result.[35]

Wisdom Principle (Reversal) Repeated (Luke 14:11; Luke 16:15)

The pivotal importance of the saying in Luke 14:11 ("Everyone who exalts himself will be humbled, and he who humbles himself will be exalted") has already been highlighted in the previous chapter of our study of Luke 14–16. The wisdom maxim echoes the language of reversal from the Magnificat and casts a long shadow across the teachings of the following chapters.[36] In its proper context, the saying targets the guests of the Phari-

---

33. Cf. Nolland, *Luke 9:21—18:34*, 831.

34. Luke 14:1–6 and Luke 6:6–11 record the only healing stories that involve the (negative) reaction of the (scribes and) Pharisees in Luke's gospel.

35. Ellis, *The Gospel of Luke*, 206, notes that this is also allusive of Jesus' resurrection.

36. An almost verbatim parallel is found in Luke 18:14, that is, at the conclusion

saical dinner, and it concerns the spheres of both human relationships and one's relationship with God.[37] To exalt oneself means ultimate abasement. The way to true exaltation is humility.[38]

An alternate version of the teaching occurs in Luke 16:15, at the conclusion of our proposed text unit. Here it is taking aim at the Pharisees, too, and it makes even more explicit the ironical tension between human value systems and divine sanction: "For what is exalted among men is an abomination in the sight of God." The reverse is left unstated, but the reader is encouraged to supply the antipode: What is despised among men may be highly valued in the sight of God (cf. 1 Cor 1:26–31!). The following parable of the Rich Man and Lazarus (Luke 16:19–31) constitutes a masterful exposé of this challenge to the Pharisees.

The brief historical sketch that Luke provides as backdrop for the saying in Luke 16:15 centers on the notion of greed ("lovers of money," Luke 16:14), and it is part of a passage (Luke 16:14–18) that functions as a literary bridge connecting the parable of the Dishonest Manager (Luke 16:1–13) with the Rich Man and Lazarus (Luke 16:19–31). Beyond this, however, the small collection of sayings performs a second, equally important task in establishing a close link between the predominantly economical imagery of chapter 16 and the contrasting notions of honor and shame (δόξα, αἰσχύνη, cf. Luke 14:9–10) in the preceding chapters, especially chapter 14.

As a result, the focus of the passage seems to shift somewhat erratically from greed to honor/shame (i.e., justifying oneself before men, being exalted among men, Luke 16:15), but this proliferation of ideas is intended to have an anaphoric effect in affording an audible joint to the dominant theme of chapter 14. Greed for money and human honor are also considered in tandem because—not unlike modern-day western conventions—"wealth was valued primarily as a means to high social position."[39] With this Luke's dual focus, the Pharisees are being portrayed as the stereotypical representatives of those who possess (or rather, love) wealth and command honor in the religious community. Although it is fair to say that the majority of Pharisees were far from being financially

---

of the last of the Lukan parables. The saying can be viewed as a hermeneutical key to virtually all of the Lukan *Sondergut*. See chapter 5 of the present study.

37. Cf. Bock, *Luke 9:51—24:53*, 1264.
38. So Morris, *Luke*, 254.
39. Tannehill, *Luke*, 249.

prominent,[40] they are held up as a warning against an antic worldly value system that is at odds with the kingdom of God.[41]

In summary, the principle of Luke 16:15 harks back to Luke 14:11 and creates a strong bond with the introduction of this complex of Lukan parables and related sayings, thus helping to define the limits of the recognizable unit (Luke 14–16). The common Lukan idiom in Luke 14:1 (ἐγένετο + ἐν τῷ + infinitive) marks a new textual unit. Thematically, the complex begins with a challenge to the Pharisaical dinner society and ends with a similar charge targeting the same group. The passage has closure, and the fact that even chapter 15 is informed by Jesus' controversy with the religious leaders (cf. Luke 15:1–2) gives this section a solid grounding.

This is also one of the reasons why I would not include Luke 17:1–10 as part of our text.[42] As will be shown in even more detail from the following discussion, Luke 14–16 is driven by Jesus' interaction with the opposition. With the inclusion of the parable of the Rich Man and Lazarus the exchange has reached its final denouement. Additionally, the unifying theme of banqueting and feasting so prominent in the collection of Lukan parables in chapters 14–16 has reached its ultimate stage in Luke 16:19–31 in order to disappear from view.[43] Hand in hand with this distinguishing mark, it bears repetition that the noticeable clustering of Lukan parables does not extend beyond chapter 16. The reader has to wait until Luke 18:1–14 for the next (and final) grouping of two such stories.

INTERNAL TEXTUAL COHERENCE

Having defined the outer limits of our text, additional evidence demonstrating the integrity of Luke 14–16 as a whole is needed to cement the idea of a conscious effort on the part of the author in presenting the

---

40. Cf. Sanders, *Judaism*, 13.

41. Therefore, Luke's portrait is not necessarily historically accurate, as one does not have to be wealthy to qualify as a "lover of money" (φιλάργυροι, Luke 16:14). Pace Tannehill, *Luke*, 249.

42. A new historical setting "between Samaria and Galilee" (Luke 17:11), indicates that Luke 17:11ff. is even more clearly removed from the parable of the Rich Man and Lazarus.

43. Even though Luke 17:7–10 speaks of "reclining at table" (Luke 17:7), the image here is clearly not one of a banquet or a dinner with guests.

The Heart of the Lukan Gospel: Luke 14–16

material as a unified textual body. The textual integrity of the complex arises from the fact that Luke 14–16 has been arranged to read as one continuing argument with several evolutions and a climax in the parable of the Rich Man and Lazarus. Its backbone consists in Jesus' alternating interaction with the Pharisees (and scribes) and his followers, with Luke's emphasis being on Jesus' rejoinders to his opponents. The nuances of this twin exchange are the subject of the following remarks.

Luke's travel narrative (Luke 9:51—19:44) includes four texts which bring Jesus' sharp criticism of the Pharisees into focus (Luke 11:37ff.; Luke 14:1ff.; Luke 15:1ff.; Luke 16:14ff.).[44] The harangue in Luke 11:37–54, shot through with several woes pronounced against the Pharisees and lawyers, certainly presents the most acid sarcasm Luke's gospel has to offer.[45] This leaves us with Luke 14–16 as the only section in the gospel featuring a sustained interest in Jesus' polemic interaction with the Pharisees.

The structure and arrangement of the text can be conceived in terms of an alternating pattern of proposition to and response by Jesus' addressees. Viewed from a distance, Luke 14–16 breaks down as follows:

Luke 14:1–24	Jesus interacts with Pharisees
Luke 14:25–35	Teaching addressed to disciples
Luke 15:1–32	Jesus interacts with Pharisees (and scribes)
Luke 16:1–13	Teaching addressed to disciples
Luke 16:14–31	Jesus interacts with Pharisees

At two junctions the setting changes (Luke 14:25; Luke 15:1), but Luke has left sufficient clues for the reader to appreciate the integrated nature of the text as a whole. First of all, the repetition of key words creates the seams that hold the various units together. In Luke 14:25–26, the saying

---

44. Note that Luke 17:20–21 does not qualify as criticism. Jesus is merely correcting a misunderstanding about the character of the kingdom of God held by virtually all, including the disciples (cf. Acts 1:6). In its literary context, Jesus' words of the present reality of the kingdom give rise to teachings on the futurist aspect of the kingdom (Luke 17:22–37. In any case, the passage does not bear the mark of a controversy. The same goes for Luke 13:31–35, since here it is not the Pharisees but Herod who is the immediate target of Jesus' words. The lament over Jerusalem (Luke 13:34–35) by no means issues an exclusive address to the Pharisees.

45. The harshness of the accusations is rivaled only by a brief invective against the scribes in Luke 20:45–47.

about renouncing (or rather, hating) one's "wife" (γυνή) looks back to the parable of the Great Banquet, where one of the original invitees absents himself on the grounds of having married a "wife" (γυνή, Luke 14:20). Jesus' instruction to the disciples (Luke 14:25–35) also harmonizes with the preceding parable on a thematic level, since in both cases proper (or, improper) prioritization identifies the main concern.[46]

Jesus' exchange with the Pharisees (and scribes) resumes in Luke 15:1ff., and once again, Luke has tied this new sub-unit to the preceding pericope with the help of verbal linkage. Jesus' invitation to "hear" ("He who has ears to hear, let him hear," Luke 14:35) occurs in immediate proximity to the remark that tax collectors and sinners were gathering to do just that, namely, to "hear" him (Luke 15:1).[47]

From here on, the Pharisees, mentioned in Luke 15:2, will keep company with Jesus, inasmuch as Luke 16:14 indicates that they were still listening to Jesus' parable of the Dishonest Manager and the following instructions about "Mammon."[48] In these ways, then, Luke has created a homogenous textual unit reaching from Luke 14:1 to the conclusion of the parable of the Rich Man and Lazarus (Luke 16:19–31), at which point the Pharisees will—for the time being—vanish from the scene.[49]

By now focusing more specifically on the *content* of Luke 14–16, the contours of the text stand out in even bolder relief. Conceived in such terms, the complex evinces the following pattern:

Luke 14:1–24	(Pharisees) Invitation & Rejection: Banquet
Luke 14:25–35	(Disciples) Hating All (. . . or you *cannot* be my disciple)
Luke 15:1–32	(Pharisees) Reception & Rejection: Banquet
Luke 16:1–13	(Disciples) Making Friends (. . . you *cannot* serve God . . .)
Luke 16:14–31	(Pharisees) Reception & Rejection: Heaven

46. Cf. Tannehill, *Luke*, 235.

47. Cf. Green, *The Gospel of Luke*, 570.

48. Nolland (*Luke 9:21—18:34*, 796–97) notes that throughout Luke 15:1—16:31 both disciples and Pharisees remain present. Accordingly, the καί in Luke 16:1 is properly rendered "also": "He *also* said to the disciples . . . "

49. Even though Luke 17:1 begins with the familiar phrase, "And he said to his disciples" (cf. Luke 16:1), mention of the "apostles" (Luke 17:5) and topographical references (Luke 17:11) will soon indicate that the above close-knit sequence of response and proposition has been abandoned.

The Heart of the Lukan Gospel: Luke 14–16

All of the sub-units addressing the Pharisees show a contrast of reception/ invitation and rejection. Thus, the triad of parables targeting the Pharisees (Great Banquet, The Lost, Rich Man and Lazarus) share a common thematic tendency centering on the notion of hospitality and meals.[50] All three also harmonize in that their cast of characters includes "anti-disciples" who are held up as a warning against sinful rejection of host (Great Banquet), brother (The Lost), and neighbor (Rich Man and Lazarus).[51]

As for the sub-units addressed to Jesus' followers, we note that they feature teachings that appear to endorse certain paradoxes. On the one hand, the disciples are taught to reject ("hate," Luke 14:26) the nearest and dearest and set no store even by their own life. Their love for their master must be such that even the closest of earthly commitments are hatred by comparison.[52] On the other hand, his followers are told to "make friends" for themselves "by means of unrighteous Mammon" (Luke 16:9).[53] The derogatory phrase involving the Aramaic transliterate "Mammon" (μαμωνᾶς, "property, wealth") asks the disciples to use what is otherwise set up as a rival god (cf. Luke 16:13) to "purchase" new friendships and ultimately gain access to "eternal dwellings" (Luke 16:9). The twin motto emerging from this comparison is to risk "losing" relationships (even family relations) and to gain new ones.

In both cases, Jesus concludes his teaching with memorable definitive sayings featuring the negated verb δύναμαι: "One *cannot* be my disciple" (Luke 14:33) is the stark alternative for failing to renounce all that one has. By the same token, a similar either/or decision is required in Luke 16:13: "One *cannot* serve two masters . . . You *cannot* serve God (and Mammon)." The two passages couched between Jesus' exchanges with the Pharisees are thus interwoven with each other by ending in a recognizable symphonic refrain.[54]

---

50. Green (*The Gospel of Luke*, 568–69) recognizes this common theme in the parabolic material of Luke 14–16.

51. It must be said, though, that the inclusion of an "anti-disciple" is not uncommon in the rest of the Lukan parables (cf. Good Samaritan, Rich Fool, Pharisee and Tax Collector).

52. Morris, *Luke*, 258.

53. Jewish sources distinguish "false Mammon" and "true Mammon" on the basis of whether wealth is acquired in honest or dishonest ways. Jesus appears to imply that in this world wealth will always be abused in some sense. Cf. Fitzmyer, *The Gospel According to Luke (x–xxiv)*, 1109.

54. In Luke 14:25–35 the phrase "cannot be my disciple" occurs no fewer than three times (Luke 14:26, 27, 33). Luke 16:13 shows the negated δύναμαι twice.

At the Heart of Luke

The characterization of the Pharisees throughout chapters 14–16 is also remarkable in that their reaction to Jesus' teachings grows worse by degrees as the tension rises. At first, Luke has them watching him carefully (Luke 14:1), certainly not with goodwill. After Jesus' initial verbal tackle (Luke 14:3–6), they remain silent for their inability to mount a serious challenge to Jesus' searching questions. In the second encounter (Luke 15:1–2), their silence has now turned into a "grumbling"[55] remark: "This fellow receives sinners and eats with them" (Luke 15:2). Finally, after having listened to Jesus' discourse on the use of wealth (Luke 16:1–13), the full force of their invidiousness is unleashed in the phrase, "they ridiculed him" (Luke 16:14). From the silent gnawing of teeth to murmuring accusations to open ridicule, the Pharisees' opposition to Jesus rises steadily to its full gusto. Their going from bad to worse in a three-step movement is an integral feature of Luke's portrait of the Pharisees in chapters 14–16 and serves to enhance the effect of a well-rounded, definable text unit with a notable climax. The parable of the Rich Man and Lazarus as Jesus' final response to the flagrant hostility delivers a worthy closure to this central section of Luke's gospel.[56] Heaven and Hades, respectively, are the ultimate expectation for both friend and foe of Jesus, and neither are revocable.

A third perspective on Luke 14–16 may now be offered, focusing on what Jesus' teachings reveal about the character of God and the disciple. Accordingly, the text block shows as follows:

Luke 14:1–24	God's Character: Mercy (exalting the outcasts) & Severity
Luke 14:25–35	Disciple's Character: Wisdom (adding up the costs)
Luke 15:1–32	God's Character: Mercy (seeking/receiving the lost)
Luke 16:1–13	Disciple's Character: Wisdom (giving away money)
Luke 16:14–31	God's Character: Severity & Mercy (exalting the outcast)

---

55. The same verb "to grumble" (διαγογγίζω) surfaces in the account of Jesus' reception of Zacchaeus the tax collector (Luke 19:7). Here, however, the reaction is not limited to one group, as the text indicates that "they *all* grumbled . . . "

56. There is no doubt that the final parable (Luke 16:19–31) with its ominous conclusion for the rich man is coined to apply the ultimate "blow" to the Pharisees, who had just been characterized as "lovers of money" (Luke 16:14). The parable introducing the human faces of wealth and poverty and their respective fate aims at the malignant agenda of Jesus' antagonists. Cf. Ringe, *Luke*, 217.

The Heart of the Lukan Gospel: Luke 14–16

The three sub-units dealing with Jesus' interaction with the Pharisees have a unifying motif in that they tend to be revelatory of God's character.[57] While both the first and the closing text highlight mercy alongside of severity,[58] only the parables of the Lost (chapter 15) evince a singular focus on God's mercy in seeking out and receiving sinners. The unmistakable emphasis on mercy at the center of Luke 14–16 is a well-calculated arrangement on the part of the author. As it stands, the parable of the Prodigal Son as the conclusion of the triad of stories in chapter 15 is the only open-ended anecdote in the collection with no overtly bad news for the establishment. It leaves the reader with the question of whether the elder son will eventually undergo a change of heart in order to join the festivities surrounding the return of the prodigal brother. As Wenham rightly observes, "Jesus has in mind his critics who also claimed to be righteous . . . and in tune with God, but whose rejection of Jesus and his ministry to sinners showed how far they were from the God they claimed to serve."[59] The controversy between Jesus and the Pharisees now stands on the razor's edge as the Pharisees are being issued a gracious invitation to join God's salvific work in Jesus' ministry. It is a moment of fragile possibilities.

The open-ended state of affairs, however, is unstable, and an answer to the question, "Will they change?" is almost expected. The pendulum swings, and the answer comes in the form of the parable of the Rich Man and Lazarus. In this final tale of reversal the reader is to see the impenitent Pharisees in the rich man and his brothers who have "Moses and the Prophets" (Luke 16:29) and yet refuse to listen to them.[60] Hence,

---

57. Forbes (*God of Old*, 279ff.) argues that this characteristic lies at the heart of virtually all of the Lukan parables. Accordingly, the parables are not only used positively to depict God's heart, but function as correctives to the views of God's character held by first century Jews. Forbes certainly advances a convincing case, but it must be noted that the Lukan parables also reveal a wealth of information about discipleship, or rather, the character of the "quintessential" disciple. The parable of the Dishonest Manager (Luke 16:1–13) may serve as a telltale example of this trait of the Lukan parables.

58. The two parables arguably convey an inverted focus on the two divine character traits. While the Great Banquet has a stronger pull towards mercy (exaltation of the outcasts), the Rich Man and Lazarus is more negative in its emphasis on the finality of judgment.

59. Wenham, *The Parables of Jesus*, 113.

60. See above n56.

the mounting hostility of the Pharisees throughout Luke 14–16[61] is set against the backdrop of Luke 15 with its marvelous revelation of the loving heart of God and so shown to be even more monstrous. Judgment is all that remains, and the concluding parable moves the plot to the inevitable denouement.

The two intervening passages (Luke 14:25–35; Luke 16:1–13) shift the attention to discipleship and are in this sense descriptive of the character of the disciple of Jesus. It is noteworthy that calculation informs both pericopes, which is intimated in the imagery of adding up the costs (Luke 14:25–35) and reducing debts (Luke 16:1–13), respectively. In the case of the parable of the Dishonest Manager the key theme of wisdom that unifies both sub-units is even stated: The dishonest manager is commended for his savvy response to the crisis ("he handled himself shrewdly," φρονίμως ἐποίησεν, Luke 16:8). Both passages answer the question, "What must I do to succeed?" They, therefore, stand in stark contrast to the rest of the material in Luke 14–16, where God's activity (revelatory of his character) in bringing about reversal takes center stage.

As has been argued so far, Luke 14–16 constitutes an artistic literary unit with its own plot and supporting structure at the heart of the travel narrative (Luke 9:51—19:44). As such, it functions as an exposition of the two main themes of reversal from Mary's Magnificat (Luke 1:51–53).

---

61. See the above discussion.

3

Exposition

Since a theological and textual framework has been established, a thorough analysis of the individual sub-units in Luke 14–16 can now be undertaken. Still, the constraints of space and relevance for the present study demand selectivity in terms of the material to be covered. Matters of authenticity have already been discussed in a general way in the introduction to this work, and I hope to remain true to my commitment to focus on the present text as it stands. Similarly, text-critical issues will be relegated to footnotes, unless they are pertinent to the exposition. The same goes for linguistic concerns. I may anticipate, too, that textual variants hardly do affect the meaning of interpretation of any of the pericopes in Luke 14–16.

Whereas chapter 2 dealt with somewhat larger sub-divisions,[1] the textual analysis of the present chapter works with smaller units, so as to allow for greater attention to exegetical detail. As a result, Luke 14:1–14 appears as an individual sub-unit, and is itself broken up into Luke 14:1–6 (the miracle story) and the collection of sayings of Luke 14:7–14. Jesus' rebuke of the Pharisees in Luke 16:14–18, which serves as an introduction

---

1. For example, Luke 14:1–14 (Introduction) and Luke 14:15–24 (Great Banquet) were considered as a single unit due to their common emphasis on Jesus' exchange with the host's (a Pharisee) guests at the dinner. In the same way, the transition of Luke 16:14–18 has been viewed in conjunction with the parable of the Rich Man and Lazarus (Luke 16:19–31), since the story is clearly triggered and informed by the foregoing debate between the two parties.

to the parable of the Rich Man and Lazarus (Luke 16:19–31), will also appear under its own heading.

INTRODUCTION: EXALTATION AND HUMILIATION (LUKE 14:1–14)

In this section Luke's initial historical notice (Luke 14:1) furnishes the stage for Jesus' continuous interaction with the Pharisees (and scribes) throughout chapters 14–16. But the dinner occasion at the home of the eminent Pharisee (Luke 14:1–6) is more than a convenient literary set-up for the series of contentions that are to follow. The pericope also serves as an important introduction to the theological concerns that govern that text block. These concerns are then distilled into the paradigmatic saying of Luke 14:11, a proverb that not only summarizes the teachings found in Luke 14:7–14, but carries significance as a thematic signpost for the rest of the material assembled in Luke 14–16.

Luke 14:1–6: Healing on the Sabbath

The healing miracle at the house of a ruler of the Pharisees connects with the following three chapters in the gospel, since banqueting will be one of the main common themes of Luke 14–16. Already in Luke 7:36 and Luke 11:37 Jesus had accepted invitations to dine at Pharisees' homes. On this occasion, however, Luke adds a reference to "one Sabbath" (Luke 14:1), which warrants some more specific comments.

Sabbath healings appear to have been common enough in Jesus' ministry,[2] but they are freighted with added theological significance in Luke's biography. Jesus' inaugural sermon in Nazareth (Luke 4:16–30) declared the "year of the Lord's favor" (Luke 4:19),[3] a reference to Isaiah's prophecy (Isa 61:1–2) anchored in the levitical legislation of the Jubilee code (Lev 25:8–17) and the Sabbath year (Lev 25:1–7). The primary purpose of the Jubilee year was the release of Jewish slaves and the restoration of the poor in their return to their original homestead. The biblical subtext to the Jubilee thus spells a dramatic turn from bondage and

---

2 Cf. Matt 12:1–4; Mk 3:1–6; Luke 6:6–11; Luke 13:10–17; John 5:1–17; John 9:1–14.

3. See the brief discussion in chapter 1.

Exposition

poverty to freedom and patrimonial recovery,[4] which comports well with the (positive) inversions contemplated in the Magnificat (Luke 1:51–53). Jesus' words in Luke 4:16–21 announce the eschatological fulfillment of these concepts.

The Sabbath year and the Jubilee (in effect, a "Sabbath of Sabbaths") were an extension of the Sabbath itself, and it is no secret that the celebration of the seventh day was a sign of reversal, namely, Israel's release from slavery (Deut 5:15) and their constitution as a nation of kings and priests under Yahweh's lordship (Exod 19:6).[5] The very fact that Jesus' declaration regarding the fulfillment of the Jubilee (Luke 4:16–21) occurred on a Sabbath day (Luke 4:16) is hardly a matter of coincidence.[6] In the words of the OT quotation, the "Sabbath of Sabbaths" centered on bringing liberty to captives, the recovery of sight, and the release of the oppressed and poor—precisely the kinds of things that Jesus demonstrated in his healing miracles on Sabbath days. There was no day more appropriate than the Sabbath to reveal God's salvific intention involving a dramatic reversal of conditions for the suffering people of God in an eschatological exodus.

When therefore Jesus had a history of performing healings on the Sabbath, it may well have been because he was conscious of the theological significance of the seventh day. His healings on the Sabbath were signs of release and rest, the very principles promoted in the institution of the Sabbath and the Jubilee, which pointed to the messianic age.[7] Since Luke's record of Jesus' inaugural sermon in Nazareth (Luke 4:16–21) assumes programmatic character in the gospel, his five Sabbath miracles (Luke 4:31–37; Luke 4:38–39; Luke 6:6–11; Luke 13:10–17; Luke 14:1–6) gain

---

4. Cf. Sloan, *The Favorable Year*, 6–7.

5. In some sense, the Sabbath was a sign of God's rule, and the command to image Yahweh by keeping the Sabbath implies Israel's participation in God's rule. Cf. Dempster, *Dominion and Dynasty*, 103. Adam refers to the Sabbath as "a participation in God's . . . rest, and also a participation in redemption." Cf. *Hearing God's Words*, 150.

6. Green draws attention to this point (*The Gospel of Luke*, 524). We may add to this Luke's choice to have Jesus' inaugural sermon in Nazareth followed by a flurry of healings which occurred on the Sabbath (Luke 4:31–39). Luke's reference to "sundown" in Luke 4:40 presumably refers to the same day, thus showing Jesus closing out the Sabbath by putting on a "fireworks" of healing and exorcisms (Luke 4:40–41). All of these signs performed on the Sabbath made visible God's salvific intention of introducing the kingdom of heaven conceived in terms of dramatic reversals. Luke's arrangement reinforces Jesus' message of the favorable year of the Lord (Luke 4:16–21).

7. So Laniak, *Shepherds*, 188.

special status as extensions of Luke 4:16–21.[8] They are pictures of the eschatological reversal that inheres the "year of the Lord's favor" and the reversal imagery of the Magnificat (Luke 1:51–53).[9]

Based on these considerations, the healing of the man on the Sabbath (Luke 14:1–6) is more than a convenient opening to Luke 14–16. The idea of reversal lies just beneath the surface of the reference to the day, and the miracle is itself a dramatic turnabout for the suffering person. In this sense, the episode functions as a trajectory for the thematic emphases of Luke 14–16.

The principle of reversal works in both directions. Not only is the sick man restored, but the Pharisees also suffer a comprehensive defeat. Although Luke 13:17 is more explicit in mentioning the adversaries "being put to shame," the reference to the opponents' silence (Luke 14:4) and their being dumbfounded (Luke 14:6) rings out the word of their humiliation after this fifth and final Sabbath healing in the gospel.[10] In particular the Magnificat's language of "confounding the proud in the thoughts of their hearts" (Luke 1:51b) resonates with Luke's reference to Jesus' opponents' inability to step up to the challenge and find an appropriate retort.

The opposition's malicious intent has already been noted in Luke 14:1 ("they were watching him carefully").[11] Jesus' question about the lawfulness of healing on the Sabbath (Luke 14:3) penetrates the Pharisees' game plan. Irrespective of whether the man suffering from dropsy had been deliberately planted, they were watching him because they held that miraculous performances on the Sabbath would constitute a violation of the law.[12] Healing the man would thus have branded Jesus as a

---

8. Luke includes five Sabbath healings of a total of seven in the NT. Luke 4:31–37; 4:38–39; and 6:6–11 have Synoptic parallels, while 13:10–17 and 14:1–6 are unique to the third gospel. John records two such miracles (5:10; 9:14). Therefore, Luke is keen on preserving a more concentrated memory of these special events in the ministry of Jesus than his peers.

9. In Luke 13:16, the connection between miracle and Sabbath as a release from bondage is especially acute (οὐκ ἔδει λυθῆναι ἀπὸ τοῦ δεσμοῦ τούτου τῇ ἡμέρᾳ τοῦ σαββάτου).

10. Cf. Just, *Luke 9:51—24:53*, 571. Just sees a steady progression from anger (6:11) to humiliation (13:17) "and now silence" (14:4) in the three Sabbath healings in Luke's account.

11. Cf. Gooding, *According to Luke*, 264; Kilgallen, *A Brief Commentary*, 146.

12. In Luke 13:14 this position is made explicit by the ruler of the synagogue, and it is implicit in the scene at the Pharisee's home.

"law-breaker."[13] However, their original agenda to find something worthy of accusations in Jesus ends in a baffling reprimand with plenty of witnesses to savor their humiliation during this significant social occasion.[14]

Jesus' question about the lawfulness of healing also entails another pertinent complex of ideas, namely that of power and oppression. The Lukan Jesus is not a politically resistant social critic, as some would have it,[15] and it would certainly be misleading to argue that "Luke's theology has been largely motivated by the social and political forces operating upon his community."[16] Luke's portrait of Jesus and the message of his account is not devoid of social-political concerns, but his conceptualization of power and oppression is at heart spiritual (or rather, theological) and eschatological. To be sure, abuse of power and oppression can and do take the form of political oppression and economic injustice, but these phenomena are ultimately rooted in a theological conflict between the Lord and his enemies. Socio-economic and political issues must be seen against Luke's eschatological framework to avoid the danger of reducing Luke's message to social ethics and the Jesus of the third gospel to little more than a political activist.[17]

At any rate, in Luke 14:1–6, the author's concern with power and oppression as a predominantly *religious* concept is overt, particularly when read alongside of the proximate account of the woman's healing in Luke 13:10–17.[18] Here suffering is conceived as an expression of satanic oppression (ἣν ἔδησεν ὁ σατανᾶς, Luke 13:16), and the logic of Jesus' rebuttal involves an *a fortiori* argument: If ordinary care is reasonably extended even to animals, then healing on a Sabbath is all the more appropriate.[19] Jesus' analogy in Luke 14:5 not only exposes the Pharisees'

13. Gooding, *According to Luke*, 264.
14. Cf. Culpepper, *The New Interpreter's Bible, Luke–John*, 284.
15. Cf. Cassidy, *Jesus, Politics, and Society*; Esler, *Community and Gospel*.
16. Cf. Esler, *Community and Gospel*, 223.
17. Bovon voices a similar caution, *Luke the Theologian*, 547.
18. All three Sabbath healings in the third gospel bear close resemblance to each other. Luke 6:9 forms a strong bond with 14:4,6. In both texts the audience can offer no answer and remains silent (ἡσυχάζειν, Luke 14:4). Cf. Marshall, *The Gospel of Luke*, 579. Likewise, the two miracles are preceded by searching questions about the "lawfulness" (ἔξεστιν, 6:9; 14:3) of healing on the Sabbath. In Luke 13:10–17 the order is reversed, in that the healing occurs first, and a set of rhetorical questions follow (13:15–16). The pericope is rounded off with a note on the shame of the adversaries (13:17), which I take to imply their inability to mount a response.
19. In the case of Luke 13:16, healing on the Sabbath is even a matter of "necessity"

hypocrisy,[20] but heightens the sense of urgency. Showing compassion on the Sabbath is not merely "lawful," but in fact becomes a matter of necessity, and any delay would be as absurd as leaving one's son in the pit.[21] Although Jesus does not speak of necessity, his analogy of situations of emergency certainly connects with his earlier reference to what is "*necessary*" on the Sabbath (Luke 13:16). Viewed in this light, the healing cannot wait *because* it is the Sabbath. Suffering *per se* does not only demand an immediate response, but this very day is a divinely appointed sign of the eschatological reversal,[22] and Jesus is, after all, "Lord of the Sabbath" (Luke 6:5). Doing what he does on the Sabbath is in keeping with the *spirit* of the law and its divine Author.

The Pharisees are not only shown to miss the subtle theological point, but their hardened attitude fosters the prolonging of "oppression" (cf. Luke 13:16) and suffering and thus stands in the way of God's salvation for Israel. In a truly grotesque sense, the religious officials become part of the problem (i.e., oppression), and they employ the law (or rather, their interpretation of the law) as a tool for keeping the man in bondage, if only for one day.[23] Torah, the spirit of which has been distilled into the commandment of love as early as Luke 10:25–37,[24] becomes the means of perpetuating the abuse of power. Jesus brings deliverance from such oppression.

(cf. ἔδει). Jesus' words very likely connect with Luke 4:16–21 and the concept of the "Sabbath of Sabbaths." To set the woman at liberty from oppression on the Sabbath is a further sign of Jesus' ministry as a fulfillment of God's promise of salvation.

20. There is some textual uncertainty in Luke 14:5. Some manuscripts (a, K, L, Ψ) have a reference to a "donkey," rather than a "son" (M, P45, P75, A, B). The "son" appears to be the more difficult reading, and is to be preferred. The urgency of helping the son/ox on the Sabbath is thus applied to the sick man.

21. Marshall, following Alford, argues that Jesus' words contain "an unexpressed *a fortiori* argument from what *men* do on the Sabbath to what *God* does" (*The Gospel of Luke*, 580).

22. Bock's contention that "even on the day of rest there is no cessation of compassion" does not go far enough and tends to ignore the text's connection to Luke 4:16–21 and its theological implications. Cf. *Luke 9:51—24:53*, 1259. Green (*The Gospel of Luke*, 548), on the other hand, recognizes the "salvific purpose of God resident in the Sabbath." He concludes that the Sabbath in Luke's gospel is "the day of divine benefaction for the needy."

23. A similar concern surfaces in Luke 16:16–18. This passage marks the final showdown between Jesus and the Pharisees in Luke 14–16. The thematic correspondence with Luke 14:1–6 adds internal coherence to Jesus' conflict with the religious leaders in the text block.

24. Cf. Nolland, *Luke 9:21—18:34*, 578.

Exposition

The above discussion of the introductory pericope of Luke 14:1–6 has shown that the themes of reversal from the Magnificat (Luke 1:51–53) are well within view of Luke's account of Jesus' healing on the Sabbath. The reference to the day is itself freighted with theological significance, which becomes ocular in the healing of the man suffering from dropsy. By the same token, the dumbfounding of the Pharisees completes the inversion pertinent to the eschatological program of the gospel. In the words of the Magnificat, God has "exalted those of humble estate" (Luke 1:52b) and "has scattered the proud in the thoughts of their hearts; he has brought down the mighty from their thrones" (Luke 1:51–52a). The exodus is underway.

Luke 14:7–14: The Principle of Reversal

The historical setting or this episode remains the same as in Luke 14:1–6, namely, Jesus' dining in the house of one of the rulers of the Pharisees on a Sabbath. Accordingly, his sage instruction is directed at his adversaries, the "lawyers and Pharisees" of Luke 14:3. The twin theme of exaltation and humiliation will now move to the front of the text's concern and will be augmented by the closely related bipolar concept of honor and shame.

Luke 14:7–11 targets the guests of the occasion, while Luke 14:12–14 is addressed to the host of the banquet, but topical affinity along the lines of rejection-replacement pattern as well as rigid formal parallelism reveal the author's intention to combine the two short instructional units into a single complex.[25] The rationale for this will be discussed below. The structural unity can be made more accessible when presented in twin columnar panels:[26]

---

25. The structural correspondences have been noted and analyzed by several commentators. Cf. Braun, *Feasting*, 43; Nolland, *Luke 9:21—18:34*, 748; Just, *Luke 9:51—24:53*, 572; Hendrickx, *The Parables of Jesus*, 112, etc.

26. I am particularly indebted to Just's analysis (*Luke 9:51—24:53*, 572).

At the Heart of Luke

Luke 14:7–11	Luke 14:12–14
Improper Behavior 7—He said to them (ἔλεγεν δὲ + καλέω) 8—When . . . do not recline . . . lest (ὅταν . . . μὴ κατακλιθῇς . . . μήποτε)	**Improper Behavior** 12—He said to them (ἔλεγεν δὲ + καλέω) 12—When . . . do not invite . . . lest (ὅταν . . . μὴ φώνει . . . μήποτε)
Proper Behavior 10—But when . . . recline . . . last place (ἀλλ' ὅταν . . . ἀνάπεσε . . . ἔσχατον τόπον)	**Proper Behavior** 13—But when . . . invite the poor . . . (ἀλλ' ὅταν . . . κάλει πτωχούς)
Promotion 10—You will be honored (ἔσται σοι δόξα)	**Promotion** 14—You will be blessed (μακάριος ἔσῃ)
Eschatological Rational 11—Reversal: Exaltation/Humiliation (ὑψόω / ταπεινόω)	**Eschatological Rational** 14—Reward: Resurrection (ἀναστάσις τῶν δικαίων)

The eschatological rationale concluding each panel may explain why Luke calls Jesus' instruction a "parable" (Luke 14:7). The teaching implies a second level of meaning, in that the words, which at first sight seem to aim at dinner etiquette, afford an analogy to the attitude prerequisite for the eschatological banquet.[27]

The scene in Luke 14:7–11 has often been seen as reflecting the custom of the *symposium* in the ancient Mediterranean world.[28] However much credence one is willing to concede to the Hellenistic *symposium* as furnishing Luke with a paradigm for this story, it is clear from Luke's account of Jesus' speech that conventional mealtime practices relating to seating arrangements (and invitations, Luke 14:12–14) were a socially constructed reality. The quality of one's seat vis-à-vis the host functioned as a barometer of one's social prestige.[29] Rank and honor is certainly the issue at the meal and Jesus' proverbial admonition about the guests' celerity in claiming the honored positions is revelatory of both their character and ultimate expectation. True honor cannot be taken, but must be bestowed.

---

27. Cf. Fitzmyer, *Luke X–XXIV*, 1045; Tannehill, *Luke*, 229.

28. So, for example, Braun, *Feasting*, 43; Ellis, *The Gospel of Luke*, 192; W. Grundmann, *Das Evangelium nach Lukas*, 290. On Luke and the *symposium*, see also Steele, "Luke 11:37–54," 379–94.

29. Bock, *Luke 9:51—24:53*, 1263.

Exposition

The backbone of Jesus' teaching reflects proverbial wisdom (Prov 25:6–7; cf. also Sir 3:17–20).[30] The sapiential advice about the pitfalls of securing one's prestige, rather than to wait for promotion, is then summarized in the aphorism of Luke 14:11. The saying demonstrates that Jesus is not primarily concerned with the honor code of Greco-Roman society, but with the standards of God's society. "Everyone who exalts himself will be humbled, and he who humbles himself will be exalted" turns the honor system of his contemporaries on its head.[31] The passive voice (ταπεινωθήσεται, ὑψωθήσεται), while not necessarily true in human affairs, indicates God's action of eschatological reversal. God bestows status by exalting the humble, and he demolishes the status of those who seek status for themselves. The Magnificat's verdict about the powerful and privileged and the underprivileged (Luke 1:52) overtly comes into view.

The concept of reversal has a rich sapiential subtext (Prov 15:33: "The fear of the Lord is instruction in wisdom, and before honor comes humility;" Prov 18:12: "Before destruction a man's heart is haughty, but humility comes before honor"). However, the maxim of Luke 14:11 also echoes Ezek 21:26.[32] This text announces the prince of Israel's demotion ("exalt what is low, humble what is exalted")[33], whose ruin consists in the removal of the crown. If Jesus was thinking of Ezekiel's castigations of Zedekiah, his maxim describing the great eschatological reversal (Luke 14:11) would have a prophetic grounding that also harmonizes with the inversion of Luke 1:52.

The address to the host of the dinner (Luke 14:12–14) targets the ethics of patronage and reciprocity, which were central to the intricate web of social relations in the Greco-Roman world.[34] The calculated *quid pro quo* of dinner occasions such as the one described in Luke 14:1–6 assumed that no gift was ever free, but came with certain strings (implicit or explicit) attached to them. The system of reciprocity demanded a repayment (ἀνταπόδομα, Luke 14:12b) in kind from one's social peers.[35]

---

30. A later rabbinic text closely resembles the teaching as well (*Lev. Rab.* 1:5).

31. Cf. Pao and Schnabel in *Commentary*, 339.

32. Ibid., 339.

33. The LXX (Ezek 21:31) reads: ἐταπείνωσας τὸ ὑψηλὸν καὶ τὸ ταπεινὸν ὕψωσας. The vocabulary of the pertinent portion of this verse evinces a striking similarity to Jesus' wisdom saying.

34. Green, *The Gospel of Luke*, 550.

35. Jesus' concern centering on reciprocation is amply communicated in the text

Consequently, generosity and hospitality conventionally cemented social status and stratification and implied a self-serving agenda. To accept an invitation obliged the guest to return the favor. A man commanding an honorable position in society, as was undoubtedly the case with Jesus' host, would therefore not invite poor folks to a dinner, since this would not only compromise one's social footing but had no promise of reciprocation. Jesus' words to the host overthrow the cultural scripts of the system of reciprocity and replace it with a new concept of eschatological reward grounded in the resurrection (Luke 14:14b).

Invitations are to be extended to the "poor, the disabled, the lame, and the blind" (Luke 14:13), rather than family, friends, and people of wealth (Luke 14:12). The sequence of unfortunate individuals is repeated verbatim in the extended guest list of the parable of the Great Banquet (Luke 14:21), which is indicative of the internal thematic coherence of Luke 14:7–24.[36] The group of nobodies with the inclusion of the "poor" is prominent in material unique to Luke's gospel.[37] It features in Luke 4:16ff. as well as the Magnificat. Jesus' words in Luke 14:12–14 echo this concern with the outcasts and entail two motions in opposite directions. By following Jesus' rule, the host would dishonor his family and the elite of society, while honoring the poor and underprivileged in their place.[38]

His identification with those of humble social rank also implies the loss of honor for the host himself—by human standards anything but a rosy prospect. In this sense, however, the wisdom saying of Luke 14:11 continues to inform the address to the host of the banquet. He is effectively told to humble himself by inviting the social pariahs. Conversely, those who extend invitations to people of high social status exalt themselves not only by putting on display their belonging to an elite, but also by advancing their personal interests in society through the prospect of reciprocation.[39] The exaltation of the humble (Luke 14:11) finally translates into the resurrection of the just (Luke 14:14b). The question regarding the precise future expectation of those who exalt themselves is, for the time being, left unanswered, except that abasement is generally anticipated (Luke 14:11).

via the cluster of words beginning with the prefix (ἀντα-/ἀντι-).
36. Cf. Hendrickx, *The Parables of Jesus*, 112.
37. Petzke (*Das Sondergut*, 133) draws attention to this point.
38. Cf. Tannehill, *Luke*, 230.
39. Ibid., 230.

Exposition

The negative counterpart to the promise of the resurrection is spelled out in the parable of the Rich Man and Lazarus (Luke 16:19–31). The rich man who refuses to feed the poor is humbled in the afterlife, the punishment of Hades (Luke 16:23). There is therefore an unmistakable correspondence between the first complex of teachings in Luke 14–16 (Luke 14:7–14) and the concluding Lazarus story (Luke 16:19–31), which helps to frame the "heart" of Luke's gospel and lends internal cohesion to the text.

We are now well positioned to make a couple of additional suggestions about Luke 14:7–14. The parallel structure of the two instructional panels[40] already urged a hermeneutical approach that allows the interpreter to see the text's message as a coalition of the two discourses of Luke 14:7–11 and Luke 14:12–14. The merger of the twin panels dovetails the twin reversal concept stated in the Magnificat and affords a satisfying introduction to Luke 14–16 as an exposition of Luke 1:51–53. The emphasis in Luke 14:7–11 is on warning those who want to be someone, that is, who seek positions of power and privilege in the world.[41] This concern generally reflects the reversal of Luke 1:51–52, resulting in the abasement of the powerful. The words of Luke 14:12–14 fit more specifically into the theme of material possessions[42] and the reversal of rich and poor as expressed in Luke 1:53. The slight shift in emphasis (which is by no means exclusive) is not only located in the mention of the rich and the poor (Luke 14:12–13), but is suggested by the language of repayment (ἀνταπόδομα, Luke 14:12b; ἀνταποδίδωμι, "to repay in full," Luke 14:14), too. The Magnificat's double reversal also beckons in the final controversy between Jesus and the Pharisees, which introduces the Rich Man and Lazarus (Luke 16:14–18). The concept is reflected in the Pharisees' self-exaltation and love of money (Luke 16:14–15) made explicit in the text.

Another closing observation about Luke 14:7–14 is in order. The two eschatological sayings that furnish the theological rationale for the required behavior (Luke 14:11, 14b) would intimate an equation of humility and righteousness. Those who humble themselves (Luke 14:11) are the "righteous" of Luke 14:14b (δικαίων) who entertain the hope of the resurrection. The combination of the two ideas will continue to reverberate throughout Luke 14–16. Thus, the Pharisees show their profound *lack* of humility by producing themselves *just* before men (cf. Luke 16:15,

---

40. See the above discussion.

41. The corresponding metaphors are the "seat/place of honor" (πρωτοκλισία, Luke 14:7–8) and the "lowest place" (ἔσχατον τόπον, Luke 14:9–10).

42. Cf. Fitzmyer, *The Gospel According to Luke X–XXIV*, 1045.

δικαιόω). The steward's lack of righteousness (ἀδικία, Luke 16:8a) becomes a reverse metaphor for wisdom and humility (Luke 16:8b–13), and the ninety-nine *righteous* mentioned in the parables of the Lost (Luke 15:7, δικαίοις) identify with those who refuse to humble themselves because they "need no repentance" (Luke 15:7).

The teaching of Luke 14:7–11 sounds the death knell for the ethics of patronage and reciprocity. The "righteous" of Luke 14:14 are therefore those whose values and worldview have been overturned and replaced by Jesus' vision of the eschatological reversal. The text remains a challenge for the contemporary readership, for one is measured against the same standard of selfless generosity and redistribution promulgated in the pericope. The challenge obtains both at the level of ultimate motives and tangible deeds.

THE GREAT BANQUET (LUKE 14:15–24)

The macarism pronounced in Luke 14:13–14 is bound to provoke a reaction, and the exclamation of the anonymous dinner guest (Luke 14:15) corresponds with the reader's expectation. The guest's words provide both a thematic and theological transition from Luke 14:1–14 to the parable of the Great Banquet. The blessedness of the "resurrection of the just" (Luke 14:14) and the banquet theme are thus linked with the blessedness of those who "will eat bread in the kingdom of God" (Luke 14:15).[43] With this introduction, the following story is raised to an eschatological level.[44]

The exclamation of Luke 14:15 does not merely expand on the theme of the eschatological banquet, but is intended to neutralize Jesus' pronouncement of blessedness on those who associate with the sorry quartet of Luke 14:13. Hendrickx cites Luke 11:27–28 as a formal parallel for the combination of a macarism with a polemical answer.[45] The words of the nameless guest also correlate with the concluding words of Luke 14:24, informing Jesus' hearers about who will *not* taste of the messianic banquet. If Luke 14:24 is seen as having an anaphoric thrust aiming back

---

43. Cf. Shillington, *Jesus and His Parables*, 184.
44. Cf. Fitzmyer, *The Gospel According to Luke X–XXIV*, 1049.
45. Hendrickx, *The Parables of Jesus*, 114. In this text, a woman in the crowd pronounces blessedness over the "womb that bore you, and the breasts that you sucked" (Luke 11:27). Jesus' reply, "Blessed rather are those who hear the word of God and keep it" (11:28), fulfills the same formal function as the parable of the Great Banquet in 14:15ff.

Exposition

at the saying of the guest, then Jesus' parable issues a counter-challenge to the claim contained in the guest's statement.

The unqualified macarism of Luke 14:15 stands in contrast with both the call to invite the underprivileged (Luke 14:13–14) and the rejection of those who refused to respond to the invitation of the master of the house (Luke 14:24). Whereas the saying of Luke 14:15 may imply that the lawyers and Pharisees who constituted the guest list of the present dinner (Luke 14:3) will certainly participate in the meal of the kingdom of God,[46] Jesus' parable takes up this implicit claim and shows that nothing is to be taken for granted without an appropriate response to the invitation to the eschatological banquet.

The parable's element of surprise, if not shock, is concentrated in both the response of the original invitees and the master's "revised" guest list. The protocols of dinner etiquette in the Mediterranean world have already been activated in Jesus' sayings in Luke 14:7–14. Invitations to meals, especially when issued by the well-to-do, signaled and promoted status in society.[47] Such occasions did not only mark those who were "in," but also drew the line between them and the disenfranchised.[48]

To snub the host of an eminent event such as is described in the story would have been an outrage in first century Palestine as elsewhere in the Greco-Roman world. The host's prestigious status in the community is unequivocally affirmed in the dinner's attribute as "grand" (δεῖπνον μέγα, Luke 14:16), the advanced position of the initial invitees, and the sheer size of the feast as indicated by the servant's vital efforts to "fill" the house (Luke 14:22–23). The host's repetitious appellation as "lord" (κύριος, Luke 14:21, 22, 23) and "householder" (οἰκοδεσπότης, Luke 14:21) can only add to the portrait of a person of a highly elevated rank in society.[49]

The original guest list accords with the advanced status of the host, a detail that would not have been lost on Jesus' listeners. At least the first two invitees are clearly characterized as persons of wealth and property.

---

46. The statement of Luke 14:15 was not made without at least some idea as to who might be included in the royal messianic banquet. Likewise, the exclamation would hardly be intended to be to the speaker's or the honored guests' detriment. It delivers a challenge to Jesus' teaching. Petzke (*Das Sondergut*, 133) argues the same point: "Damit soll die von Jesu Rede vollzogene Einschränkung der Teilnehmer am (eschatologischen) Mahl aufgehoben werden" (Thus, Jesus' speech's restriction about the participants at the [eschatological] dinner is canceled").

47. Rohrbaugh, "The Pre-Industrial City," 141.

48. Cf. Green, *The Gospel of Luke*, 555.

49. Braun, *Feasting*, 73.

At the Heart of Luke

The purchase of a field (Luke 14:18) and five yoke of oxen (Luke 14:19), respectively, distinguishes both as upper-class absentee landlords.[50] The ability of purchasing land in first century Palestine's highly stratified society was limited to a few privileged individuals. The same obtains for the second person's acquisition of ten oxen in a single transaction, when the average farmer would have owned no more than two yoke of oxen.[51] Thus, by any ancient standards, both men must be considered wealthy and constituted the kind of dinner guests one would have expected to meet at the banquet of the story's prominent host.

The newly-wed third party (Luke 14:20) seemingly departs from the pattern of accentuated wealth among the original guests. However, Braun reminds us of the fact that in antiquity even marriage was—at least in part—governed by economic considerations: "Especially among the wealthy elite, primary among motives for marriage was the generation of legitimate sons as heirs to ensure that property remained in the family. Another motive, slightly lesser perhaps, was the transaction of a large dowry (wealth) to which came attached the added benefit of a manager of household chores (labor)."[52] The overt shift from the domain of economic enterprise to familial duties, therefore, does not necessarily preclude the continuing presence of economic interests in the response of the third invitee. However one assesses the situation, the inclusion of the third party among the wealthy landowners plausibly suggests that this person too commanded considerable respect in the community. He was deemed "good company" for his illustrious peers.

Since then the feast-event is unfolding according to well-established societal conventions, and both host and guests are appropriately identified as belonging to the communal elite, why does the story take such a bizarre turn? Given the tight protocols of dinner events, why would socially privileged individuals reject the invitation of a man who is at least their equal in class? Their closing ranks in refusing to attend the banquet exposes the host to public shame and vilification, rather than the expected honor shown in their presence at the event.[53]

---

50. Ibid., 75.

51. This estimate is widely affirmed and was first stated in connection with the parable in Jeremias, *The Parables of Jesus*, 177. See also Bock, *Luke 9:51—24:53*, 1274.

52. Braun, *Feasting*, 77.

53. Cf. Snodgrass, *Stories with Intent*, 307–8.

Exposition

The three last-minute excuses offered in Luke 14:18–20 are paper-thin[54] and do not provide an adequate answer to the question, "How could they . . . ?" In fact, since none of them could possibly be considered a credible and reasonable priority, the apologies themselves pose a major social affront to the host. They have the ring of "cheap" excuses made by those who do not judge the host worthy of a more dignified and discreet response. Implicit in the absurd answers is the low rating of the host, and they describe the respondents' lives as being embedded in possessions and family relationships. The conflict of interests is shown in the use of the expression "to have need" (ἔχω ἀνάγκην, Luke 14:18) in the first excuse. It sets up an intriguing contrast with Luke 14:23. Here, the social distance between the host and the outcasts would have required the declining of the invitation. Consequently, the host has to "compel" them to enter the festivities (Luke 14:23).[55] Just as it would have been inappropriate for them to "enter" (εἰσέρχομαι, Luke 14:23) the feast, resulting in the application of "pressure" (ἀναγκάζω, Luke 14:23), so it was inappropriate for the original guest to "go out" (ἐξέρχομαι, Luke 14:18) and inspect land, claiming to act under "pressure" (ἔχω ἀνάγκην, Luke 14:18). In both cases, some form of pressure is required to override the most natural and expected response. This renders the response of the first guest (and by implication, those of his two peers) as unfit for the occasion.

Some have suggested that the excuses were modeled on Deut 20:5–7.[56] This text lists reasons for exemption from military service. If the parallel is affirmed, it would cause the excuses of the original guests to appear even more flimsy than is already the case. The scenario in the parable is, after all, not nearly as dramatic as that of warfare, thus making the call for adequate excuses all the more stringent. Yet, the situations described in Deuteronomy 20 are on the whole quite different from our story (i.e., building a house, planting a vineyard, engagement to a woman), so that the bond between the two texts is not as convincing as has been argued.[57]

---

54. Cf. Nolland's discussion in *Luke 9:21—18:34*, 753–54.

55. The group described in Luke 14:23 was just as underprivileged as the quartet of 14:21. They belonged to a different social stratus, and the fixed boundaries of society were simply not to be crossed. Cf. Braun, *Feasting*, 86–94.

56. Shillington (*Jesus and His Parables*, 185), for example, calls the parallelism "striking." He believes the connection with Deut 20:5–7 to be valid due to Luke's preoccupation with Deuteronomy in his travel narrative.

57. So Hendrickx, *The Parables of Jesus*, 117; Beale and Carson, *Commentary on the New Testament*, 340; Marshall, *The Gospel of Luke*, 588.

The question remains: How could the guests refuse the invitation of the distinguished host of the banquet and thus fail to play the game of reciprocity and social status? Nobody would have dared to snub the host in this way under the pretense of something else being more important. The parable's first element of shock hinges on the fatally skewed rating of the first-choice guests. They do not properly assess the situation, and their priorities are woefully unbalanced, even to the point of humiliating the host.

The shock of the unheard-of rejection, however, is not an end to itself. It must be seen in light of Jesus' invitation to enter the kingdom. The parable's object of comparison is the eschatological banquet in the kingdom of God (cf. Luke 14:15). "Jesus is making the point that other concerns get in the way of deciding for Jesus and sharing the hope of the eschaton."[58] The ultimate occasion is being announced, in that God himself is issuing invitations to his heavenly banquet. Participation in this meal depends on the appropriate response on the part of the invited.[59] Viewed in light of the grand event, the excuses now appear to be not only flimsy but absurd.

The identity of the first-choice guests is hinted at in the subtle shift from the third person singular in the author's initial notice (Luke 14:16) and the master's address to the servant (Luke 14:23) in the second person plural in Luke 14:24: "For I tell you all . . ." Most naturally, it is still the master of the story speaking here, but the shift in number has the effect of making him step outside the narrative world in order to directly challenge the guests at the Pharisee's home.[60] If Jesus' parable is read as a reply to the inclusive exclamation of Luke 14:15 ("Blessed is everyone who will eat bread in the kingdom of God"), then the story is narrowing down the number of guests by saying, "The privileged first-choice guests will not be there."

The Great Banquet is (in part) targeting the religious elite of Israel who forfeit the hope of the eschatological banquet by closing ranks in rejecting God's invitation.[61] This invitation to participate in the kingdom of God has already been the issue in the teachings of Jesus up to this point in Luke.

58. Bock, *Luke 9:51—24:53*, 1273.
59. Cf. Snodgrass, *Stories with Intent*, 314.
60. So Green, *The Gospel of Luke*, 555.
61. Cf. Gowler, *Host*, 246.

Exposition

The identification of the householder with God, however, has been contested. Green finds the juxtaposition of the story's authority figure with God problematic, since in that case the inclusion of the outcasts would be no more than an afterthought for God.[62] Tannehill advances a very similar argument: "The master in the parable turns to the outcasts only because he is angry at being snubbed by his social equals."[63] He comes to the conclusion that "the man is simply a man, not a representative of God."[64] To be sure, God's mercy towards the underprivileged as having top priority has been stated early on in the gospel of Luke (Luke 1:52-53; Luke 4:18ff.; Luke 6:35-36). But this appeal is found to carry less weight when the narrative sequence of Luke 14:16-24 is understood in terms of reflecting the concerns of the immediate context of the parable and the principle of reversal.

The Great Banquet does, after all, also portray a great reversal, with the high-ranked initial guests being finally rejected (Luke 14:24) and the social pariahs being received. The demotion of the group of wealthy and influential individuals contrasts with the promotion of those of low social status. The sequence of this movement on two fronts (demotion—promotion) mirrors the structure of the wisdom saying of Luke 14:11 and can ultimately be traced to the inversion of Luke 1:51-53. There is no conflict with Lukan theology.[65] The story is closely tracking the metaphor of Luke's pattern of reversal.

Before we further explore the implications of this reversal, a few comments about the addressees of the second and third invitation are in order. The poor, maimed, blind, and lame of the city (Luke 14:21) recall the list of Luke 14:13 and texts with similar vocabulary (Luke 1:51-53; Luke 4:18; Luke 6:20-23; Luke 7:22). The quartet finding itself in the home of the wealthy master thus corresponds to the humble being exalted (Luke 14:11).[66]

The third group of people has often been seen as pointing to the inclusion of the Gentiles.[67] Luke's preoccupation with this theme in

---

62. Green, *The Gospel of Luke*, 556.

63. Tannehill, *Luke*, 234.

64. Ibid., 234.

65. *Pace* Green, *The Gospel of Luke*, 556.

66. The OT subtext for this reversal of fortune is Isa 29:18-19; 35:5-6; 61:1-2.

67. Bock, *Luke 9:51—24:53*, 1277; Forbes, *The God of Old*, 107-8; Morris, *Luke*, 257; Stein, *Luke*, 394; Just, *Luke 9:51—24:53*, 557; Fitzmyer, *The Gospel According to Luke X-XXIV*, 1053; Bosch, *Die Heidenmission*, 124-31.

Luke-Acts is beyond dispute. The idea of a reference to the Gentiles also gathers some support from the fact that the ingathering of the nations and the partial rejection of Israel has been alluded to in the immediate neighborhood of our text (Luke 13:29). The pericope of the Narrow Door (Luke 13:22–30) even concludes with a reversal saying quite comparable to the one found in Luke 14:11 ("And behold, some are last who will be first, and some are first who will be last," Luke 13:30). Considering the proximity of the two passages and the overall importance of the inclusion of the Gentiles for Luke's theology, the third group (Luke 14:23) may arguably be viewed as pointing to the Gentiles.

A reference to the Gentile mission, however, is by no means certain. The statement of Luke 14:23 may just as well reflect a proper knowledge of the ancient Palestinian city.[68] Braun, following Rohrbaugh,[69] contends that the third group is representative of poor countryside peasants whose economic plight often forced them to contract with the urban elite for sordid labor. The rural peasantry was generally regarded as barbaric and uncivilized in the eyes of the aloof urban aristocracy.[70] The low status of the second group of replacement guests can therefore be seen to reinforce the parable's social reversal. Their presence at the meal of a wealthy city-dweller would have been just as eccentric and bizarre as the inclusion of the urban outcasts mentioned in Luke 14:21. By identifying the alternate guests as coming "from the wrong side not only of one, but of two solidly fixed social boundaries,"[71] Jesus' teaching continues on its collision course with cultural conventions. Thus, while a reference to the Gentiles, generally regarded as unclean by observant Jews, cannot be discounted, the introduction of the rural peasantry carries its own weight in the plot of the story. The original listeners were certainly familiar enough with the situation of those who were excluded from urban life and well-positioned to take measure of the provocative imagery of the story. A supposed allegorical allusion to the *ethical* identity of those poor peasants (i.e., Gentiles) cannot add anything to the power of the story's appeal. The point of the parable centers on the immense socio-economic distance between the first-choice guests and the two groups that take their place. The referents of the replacement groups should be identified accordingly.

---

68. Cf. Tannehill, *Luke*, 233.
69. Rohrbaugh, "The Pre-Industrial City," 144–45.
70. Braun, *Feasting*, 91.
71. Ibid., 92.

Exposition

Based upon the above discussion, we may pull together our findings in the parable of the Great Banquet to ascertain how the story contributes to the theme of reversal in Luke 14. We note first of all that the dual movement of demotion and promotion (Luke 14:11) inspires both language and form of the parable, resulting in a new social order that stands in stark contrast to the conventions currently in place. The Great Banquet is thus developing the theme of Luke 14:7–14.

When the story is read against the backdrop of Jesus' ministry, namely his call to repentance and participation in God's rule (or, God's "party"), the opting out of the invitation of the well-to-do translates into self-exaltation and pride. Not only do earthly concerns outweigh their interest in the kingdom of God,[72] but their lame excuses reveal that a seat at God's eschatological banquet is not considered a "place of honor" (cf. Luke 14:7). Thus, while the unnamed guest at the dinner pronounces everyone blessed "who will eat bread in the kingdom of God" (Luke 14:15), Jesus' parable intimates that the religious leaders of Judaism pursue a different system of priorities. Consequently, since they reject God's invitation extended via Jesus' ministry, they will not "taste" of God's banquet (Luke 14:24).

The concept of self-exaltation spells superiority and thus entails comparison and valuation. The parable of the Great Banquet explains the negative element of the reversal of Luke 14:11 in terms of one's valuation of God's kingdom. For the Pharisees (so the story suggests) the hope of the eschatological banquet is not good enough. The rejection of Jesus' invitation is parallel to the insult of turning down the host's call to come to the feast and expresses their hidden contempt for Jesus' teaching. We could say that Jesus—or ultimately God, as the host of the banquet—becomes the outcast by being spurned by the religious heavyweights. In the story, the host is being dishonored by the wealthy elite closing ranks against him. In a similar way, the religious aristocracy of Israel erects barricades that demarcate against Jesus and dishonor God. As the story goes, they will stop at nothing to silence Jesus.

The response of the disgraced host in the story translates into God's rejection of those who proudly reject him on the one hand and his identification with the lowly on the other. By compelling the poor and underprivileged to come to his banquet, God also fills the role of the ideal host of Luke 14:12–14, who invites those who cannot reciprocate. The reversal

---

72. Cf. Bock, *Luke 9:51—24:53*, 1273.

is complete. The proud are being humbled, while the have-nots are being exalted. At the same time, the exalted host of the occasion, after having been insulted by those of high status, humbles himself by feasting with the social pariahs.

The parable further reveals that God's invitation to his banquet is inclusive. Everything depends on one's response to the call. The inclusiveness of God's appeal will resurface in the concluding story of chapter 15. Here the father's love extends to both the prodigal and his stubborn brother who also refuses to attend the festivities. Significantly, in the Great Banquet the master's servant is ordered to "go out" (ἐξέρχομαι, Luke 14:23) to urge the outsiders from the countryside to "enter" (εἰσέρχομαι, Luke 14:23), while in Luke 15:28 the father himself "goes out" (ἐξέρχομαι) and resorts to imploring his son on account of his refusal to "enter" (εἰσέρχομαι).

So the main question the parable of the Banquet addresses is, "Who will attend the eschatological banquet?"[73] Sequence and plot of the story are relative to this concern. The story answers the query through the negative example of those who made up the original guest list. Only those who understand the value of the offer and respond accordingly will be present. Anything that reduces the value of the divine appeal dishonors God and, by implication, places self with its various interests above the host of the eschatological banquet. Humiliation will be the consequence. Located at the heart of the message is the system and rating of values one brings to the confrontation with the call to the kingdom. No value may compete with that of the kingdom.

Whereas this concept of valuation will be further expanded in Luke 14:25–35 in the context of discipleship, we may at this point appreciate the presence of a subtle sapiential sub-current in the parable. In Jesus' teaching of the treasure and the pearl (Matt 13:44–46), the perceived value of the kingdom of heaven is *non plus ultra* and justifies the sacrifice of anything to obtain it. The kingdom is the most prized possession one can acquire. This concept finds its OT counterpart in the wisdom literature of ancient Israel. Not only is wisdom described as a treasure (Prov 2:1–4; Wis. 7:14), but the recognition of its value as superior to any material gain makes its acquisition one's top priority (Prov 3:13–15; Prov 4:7–8, 10–27; Sir. 15:1–8; Wis. 7:7–14; Wis. 8:5). The idea of rating and valuation in the parable of the Great Banquet provides a point of contact with

---

73. Cf. Snodgrass, *Stories with Intent*, 313.

Israel's wisdom. The final rejection of the three wealthy men is a result of their placing possessions and family above the call to come to the feast. They do not recognize the value of the kingdom (banquet).

The framing of the parable of the Great Banquet is already strongly driven by wisdom themes. The teachings of Luke 14:7–11 have been lifted from Prov 25:6–7, and the aphorism of reversal (Luke 14:11) connects with Prov 29:23 and a host of other wisdom texts (cf. Prov 18:12; Prov 15:33; Sir. 1:19; Sir. 4:11; Sir. 10:14; Sir. 11:1; Wis. 10:1–2) which suggest that wisdom, when chosen as one's treasure, brings about dramatic reversal. Conversely, the spurning of wisdom precipitates inevitable decline.

Jesus' teachings in Luke 14:25–35 function as commentary on the parable of the Banquet, reinforcing the principle of proper valuation (Luke 14:26, 33). At the center of this pericope are the twin parables of the Tower-builder and the King Going to War (Luke 14:28–32). The imageries of warfare and construction with the call for wise calculation and foresight are rooted in the wisdom tradition, too (Prov 24:3–6).[74]

The parable itself, structured by the call to the banquet, bears some resemblance to personified Wisdom's invitation to feast at her table (Prov 9:1–6). In both cases servants perform the duty of summoning the guests, and even though in the parable the initial invitations are limited to the host's wealthy peers, the story as a whole suggests an open and universal appeal, as has been argued above. The tables are set, and the question is, who will respond to the call to "Come" (Prov 9:5, ἔλθατε [LXX]; Luke 14:17, ἔρεσθε).

CALCULATING THE COST OF DISCIPLESHIP (LUKE 14:25–35)

Luke's editorial choice to follow up the story of the Great Banquet with the teachings of Luke 14:25–35 draws material from a different setting (Luke 14:25) into the complex of Luke 14–16. In the preceding dinner scene Jesus was engaged in controversy with the Pharisees (Luke 14:1–24). The shift to the journey motif and the crowds who followed him sets a formal structure for the rest of our text, where the pattern of alternating audiences (Pharisees/scribes—disciples) will be consistent through Luke 16:31.[75]

---

74. Hultgren (*The Parables of Jesus*, 143) argues this point.
75. See the above discussion under 2.2., *Internal Textual Coherence*.

Although some of the material (i.e., Luke 14:26–27, 34–35) in this unit is very similar to texts found in Matthew's gospel (Matt 10:37–38; Matt 5:13; cf. also Mk 9:49–50), the Lukan "version" of these sayings still retains distinct features. While Matthew uses comparative degree (loving family *more* than Jesus, Matt 10:37–38), Luke characterizes the disciple's relationship to Jesus in absolute terms (hating family as a requirement for discipleship).[76] The two pericopes also differ in that Luke's gospel has a threefold emphasis on the inability of being a disciple (Luke 14:26, 27, 33), whereas Matthew prefers the language of unworthiness (Luke 10:37–38). The sayings could have their origin in a common source,[77] but it is equally feasible to posit variations on similar teachings used by Jesus.[78] The twin parables of the Tower Builder and the King Going to War at the center of the passage (Luke 14:28–32) have no parallel in the other gospels. In any case, the critical issue for this study is how the material interacts with the Lukan context, whether some of the verses derive from common sources or not.

The pericope has been framed by three parallel phrases that speak of discipleship as precluding certain attitudes (Luke 14:26–27, 33, οὐ δύναται εἶναί μου μαθητής), with Luke 14:34–35 forming an addendum to the teachings. In all three cases, the phrase appears in the posterior position as the apotasis of a conditional statement. The inclusion of parabolic instruction in memorable, pithy sayings is commensurate with Luke's editorial technique in other passages (cf. Fig Tree, Luke 13:6–9 in Luke 13:1–9; Unjust Judge, Luke 18:2–5 in Luke 18:1–8),[79] notwithstanding the possibility that (in some instances) the arrangement originated with Jesus' own didactic style. The framing in Luke 14:25–35 functions theologically, furnishing the interpretive grid and impetus for the twin parables (Luke 14:28–32).[80]

The back-to-back stories in turn evince an analogous structure.[81] They move from the conception of a venture to the calculation of the resources, in order to draw a conclusion about the possibility of success. Both parables close with the contemplation of a negative outcome. Thus,

---

76. Cf. Bock, *Luke 9:51—24:53*, 1281.

77. So Nolland, *Luke 9:21—18:34*, 761; Fitzmyer, *The Gospel According to Luke X-XIV*, 1060; Marshall, *The Gospel of Luke*, 591.

78. Cf. Bock, *Luke 9:51—24:53*, 1281.

79. Curkpatrick, "Parable Metonymy," 300.

80. Ibid., 300.

81. Petzke, *Das Sondergut*, 134–35.

Exposition

although Luke 14:25–35 may well be a patchwork of sayings from multiple sources, the present text possesses a fair degree of literary cohesion.

In addition to the text's internal cohesive arrangement, we note its strong nexus with the preceding material. The reference to the "wife" (Luke 14:26, γυναῖκα) in the context of weighing priorities is anaphoric of one of the excuses in the parable of the Great Banquet (Luke 14:20, γυναῖκα). More generally, the problem in both the latter story and Luke 14:25–35 is preoccupation with something other than the kingdom of God which leads to exclusion (Luke 14:24, 26–27, 33–35). Luke 14:15–24 also describes a certain disparity between the inflated expectations of the religious elite (Luke 14:15)[82] and the reality of the eschatological banquet. Similar contours are discernible in Luke 14:25–35, where the crux of the matter concerns the tension between an overly enthusiastic affirmation of discipleship and the sobering terms of it spelled out in Jesus' teachings to the crowds.[83]

The two pericopes (Luke 14:15–24, 25–35) further inform and (in some sense) complete each other via a subtle inverse focus. If the three excuses in the Great Banquet gravitate towards economic preponderance with only one of them appealing to family life, Jesus' discourse in Luke 14:25–35 transposes the point of main effort. The two conditions described in Luke 14:26–27 have been juxtaposed on account of their stress on family relations. The imagery of "bearing one's cross" (Luke 14:27) relates to the disciple's rejection by family members, even though the scope of persecution and pain exceeds the sphere of the family as the most treasured social bond. "The figure of cross-bearing denotes a willingness to bear the pain of persecution as a result of following Jesus. It is another way to express willingness to 'hate one's soul' in self-sacrifice."[84] The main emphasis of the two sayings in Luke 14:26–27 is certainly on the family. Luke 14:33, on the other hand, introduces a perspective on material attachments. The renouncing of possessions is most likely intended in terms of total allegiance to Jesus, so as to distance oneself from any idolatrous encumbrance. While in the historical context of Jesus' ministry the call to renounce all possessions had the most radical edge, requiring the actual and complete relinquishment of

---

82. See the above discussion on Luke 14:15 under chapter 3.2.
83. Talbert recognized this parallel in *Reading Luke*, 176.
84. Bock, *Luke 9:51—24:53*, 1286.

material things and business in some cases (cf. Luke 5:28),[85] the parallel with Luke 14:26–27 suggests a metaphoric meaning. Renunciation appeals to one's agenda and choices, just as "hating" one's family is a way of speaking of the total commitment Jesus demands in relation to family ties.[86] One is not to ignore the command to love one's neighbor (including family), but loving Jesus is the *sine qua non* for the follower. The disciple's ultimate allegiance is to him.

The unmistakable focus on economic concerns and the auxiliary role of family matters in the Great Banquet is noticeably reversed in Luke 14:25–35, with the result that the two texts in concert bring balance and symmetry to the larger text portion (i.e., Luke 14:15–35). At the same time, we recognize a logical progression in thought from the Great Banquet to the teachings of Luke 14:25–35, as we move from invitation to specification. The parable of the Banquet hinges on "coming to" (Luke 14:17) the festivities and is thus aiming at the cost of entering the kingdom. Jesus' teachings on discipleship (Luke 14:25–35) deal with "coming after" (Luke 14:27) Jesus and stress the cost not of entering but of maintaining an ongoing relationship. We could say that the preceding parable speaks of the fundamental decision for the kingdom, whereas Luke 14:25–35 reminds us of the need to affirm this decision and to live in accord with it.[87] Hence, despite the change of scenery and audience, the present text develops the theme of the Great Banquet and is thus integrally related to the whole discourse of Luke 14:1–24.

Another detail regarding Luke's editorial arrangement deserves mentioning at this point. The lawyers and Pharisees (Luke 14:1, 3) are Jesus' primary interlocutors in Luke 14:1–24. When this group resurfaces in the narrative seam of Luke 15:1–2, their grumbling is directed against Jesus' habit of associating with the outcasts. This complaint is *au fond* playing off the teachings of Luke 14:1–24, in which current conventions are overturned. This ligature between Luke 14:1–24 and Luke 15:1–2 further enhances the position of Luke 14:25–35 as a well integrated

---

85. So Nolland, *Luke 9:21—18:34*, 764.

86. The call to "hate" is in this sense a call to "love less" (cf. Gen 29:30–31; Deut 21:15–17). The opposite notion is present in the Great Banquet (cf. Luke 14:20), where the original dinner guests loved other things more and had themselves excused from the feast.

87. Bock (*Luke 9:51—24:53*, 1284) advances the same argument. Cf. also Marshall, *The Gospel of Luke*, 591; Green, *The Gospel of Luke*, 564; Snodgrass, *Stories with Intent*, 382.

Exposition

textual component in Luke 14–16. The theme of strained family relations in Luke 14:25–35 ("hating" one's relatives) also finds its counterpart in Luke 15:1–32 (the elder brother's rejection of both father and brother), notwithstanding the need to differentiate the causes. Luke 14:25–35 features notable topical connections with both the Great Banquet and the parables of chapter 15.

The emphasis in Luke 14:25–35, then, is on redirected loyalties, making one's relationship to Jesus the ultimate norm of life.[88] The concluding saying about salt is to be read in the same way. In this context, saltiness symbolizes the total allegiance required for disciples. Salt losing its saltiness points to deteriorating allegiance or discipleship devoid of commitment or sacrifice.[89] How is one to keep discipleship pristine? Jesus' teaching indicates that an ongoing and deliberate choice based on calculating the costs is what he demands from his followers.[90]

The language of calculation (ψηφίζω, Luke 14:28, "to count") and careful planning is the staple of the back-to-back parables in Luke 14:28–31. As mentioned above, the parables echo the wisdom tradition from Prov 24:3ff.[91] Both portray a wise person assessing expenses for a venture.[92] A wise decision entails a reasoned reflection leading to a calculated choice. The fool, on the other hand, is exposed to mockery (tower builder) and humiliation (king) because he has failed to cogitate properly. If therefore a wisdom theme was already present in Luke 14:1–24, common sense wisdom applied to discipleship now takes center stage. Wisdom involves making calculated choices. The parables move the concern of intentionality in the ongoing choice for Jesus into the realm of wisdom.

Luke 14:25–35 also points back to the wisdom saying of Luke 14:11 with its concept of reversal. The teachings about discipleship require a reorientation according to which received values, such as family relations

---

88. Stein (*Luke*, 399): "Jesus demands a position above all else in life." Morris (*Luke*, 258) cites Karris's words: "Discipleship is not periodic volunteer work on one's own terms and at one's convenience.

89. Fitzmyer, *The Gospel According to Luke X–XXIV*, 1068; Tannehill, *Luke*, 236; Marshall, *The Gospel of Luke*, 596; Wenham, *The Parables of Jesus*, 204.

90. Cf. Green, *The Gospel of Luke*, 565.

91. Hultgren draws attention to this OT text source (*Parables of Jesus*, 138). Petzke (*Das Sondergut*, 135) speaks of the stories as indicating wisdom ("Beide Beispiele zeigen Klugheit an.").

92. Snodgrass (*Stories with Intent*, 382) discerns verbal and conceptual links, "especially regarding wisdom, in the parables of the Two Builders (Luke 6:46–49) and the Ten Virgins (Matt 25:1–13)."

(Luke 14:26–27) and possessions (Luke 14:33), become secondary to one's loyalty to Jesus. The disciple is to "humble oneself" (cf. Luke 14:11b) under the cross of discipleship and in this sense experience the loss of status in the family network and in the community at large, where Jesus' teachings are not cherished. Joining a "dubious" movement existing on the fringes of Jewish society compromised the honor of one's family and brought disgrace on the disciple.[93] The same is true for "renouncing all" (Luke 14:33) for the sake of following Jesus. In this sense, following Jesus describes a scenario similar to taking a seat "in the lowest place" (Luke 14:10), for it will cost one's all. Humbling oneself in terms of status and allegiances for the sake of God's reign is unavoidable, if one is to entertain the hope of the eschatological exaltation (Luke 14:11), translating into the "resurrection of the just" (Luke 14:14). While loss and shame are (at least in part) characterizing the disciple's situation in this life, honor and exaltation are in store in the eschaton. So even though discipleship is costly and seems to entail disadvantage, this is the promising course of action. The parables of Luke 14:28–32 encourage the listener to come to the same conclusion in full view of the difficulties of siding with Jesus.

The reversal works in the opposite direction, too. Refusal to humble oneself and bring the neck under Jesus' cross will cost one's all just as well. Implied in this choice is the idea that honor and status in family and society are being retained for the sake of one's own advancement. Preferring a seat "in a place of honor" (Luke 14:8) will eventually precipitate humiliation (Luke 14:11a), since it is a choice against Jesus and the kingdom of God.

Self-exaltation is hinted at in the parables of the Tower Builder and the King Going to War. Without proper assessment, both would have an inflated opinion of their abilities and resources required for success. The respective sentiments are, "I *can* build . . . ," and, "I *can* go to war and gain victory," when neither have enough to finish.

Some interpreters see two different aspects of discipleship in the pair of parables. Longenecker, following Hunter,[94] contends that the Tower Builder is about whether one can afford to follow Jesus, while the King Going to War centers on whether one can afford to refuse Jesus' demands.[95] According to this approach, the king deciding to engage rep-

---

93. Cf. Tannehill, *Luke*, 235.
94. Hunter, *Interpreting the Parables*, 65.
95. Longenecker, *The Challenge*, 293.

resents a person who, after weighing the options, chooses to reject Jesus' "offer of peace."[96] This interpretation, while not impossible, seems less likely to express the intended meaning of the second parable. The most plausible reading of Luke 14:31–32 takes account of the text's proximity to the parable of the Tower Builder and the parallel structure characterizing the two illustrations. Both speak of the conception of a venture (building, conflict) and calculating the resources (money, troops) toward a successful conclusion of the undertaking. In the case of Luke 14:28–30, this would be the completion of the structure, despite the possibility that it might take the builder's total resources. Similarly, Luke 14:31–32 envisions a military scenario of great risk with the numerical odds being against the king. He has to commit all of his troops to the campaign, and his calculation raises the question of whether, having put everything on the line, he will be able to gain the victory. Victory spells honor, whereas defeat, capitulation, or surrender will result in humiliation and shame.[97] Thus, while both parables evince a parallel structure and convey a nearly identical message in their focus on calculating the cost of discipleship, the second one does not merely reiterate what has already been captured in the Tower Builder. Rather, it intensifies the challenge by not only raising the stakes to a national level, but by underscoring the difficulty of the venture (i.e., 2–1 numerical odds against the king) and the great danger of loss to both material and life. By the same token, discipleship is neither cheap nor without risk.

An additional aspect of intensification is present in that the king in armed conflict faces more pressure. His hand is forced, while the landowner may or may not build a tower. Both characters make a decision, but the king in Luke 14:31–32 will have to deal with his enemy, whether he engages him in combat or not. This scenario serves to highlight the inevitability of making a decision with regards to discipleship when faced with the reality of the kingdom of heaven, a notion less pronounced in the first tale.

The above-mentioned alternative reading of Luke 14:28–32 tends to deconstruct the parallelism that inheres within the twin parables. If constructing a tower and going to war harmonize in representing

---

96. Bock (*Luke 9:51—24:53*, 1289), Marshall (*The Gospel of Luke*, 594), and Just (*Luke 9:51—24:53*, 582) advocate the same view.

97. Even surrender to the enemy's "terms of peace" (Luke 14:32), while avoiding unnecessary military defeat, is a form of subjugation to the dictates of a foreign power. It is, in effect, accepting defeat without the concomitant ruin of a loss on the battlefield.

discipleship, they are the desirable choices, notwithstanding the difficulties and even danger of the proposed courses of action. Any other options, such as aborting building plans or surrender to a superior power, constitute choices that exemplify failure in discipleship. This appears to be the most natural rendering of the wisdom parables. Accordingly, following Jesus is exacting, requires sacrifice and entails risks. One must be willing to commit everything to the cause of the kingdom because there is no shortcut to authentic discipleship.

The negative aspect of reversal from Luke 14:11 (self-exaltation leading to humiliation) is reflected in Luke 14:25–35 in three consecutive images, which gradually magnify the consequences for failure in discipleship. While foolishness draws the mockery of witnesses in the parable of the Tower Builder, the king in the second parable faces destruction or, in case of surrender, subjugation in terms of taxation and whatever additional terms are imposed to make the weaker king a permanent vassal to his superior. Finally, the saying of Luke 14:34–35 portrays the would-be disciple who will not stay the course in terms of worthless salt (salt without taste). The consequence is total contempt and rejection.[98] The idea of being "thrown out" (Luke 14:35) does not only connect with the proverbial principle of Luke 14:11, but echoes the master's verdict on the original guests of the Great Banquet (Luke 14:24). They are left out and rejected. The reversal has come full term both in the case of those who refuse to respond to the call of the kingdom and in regards of halfhearted disciples who lack the requisite commitment in light of Jesus' total demands of discipleship.

One additional textual feature deserves our attention. As was the case in the parable of the Great Banquet, the pericope of Luke 14:25–35 also furnishes an open invitation. Discipleship will call for undivided loyalties, but it is open for all.[99] This concern is expressed in the language of

---

98. Marshall (*The Gospel of Luke*, 591) identifies this notion with the expectation of the eschatological judgment.

99. Hultgren (*The Parable of Jesus*, 140) argues that "discipleship . . . is not possible for everyone." But while not all will become disciples, there appears to be no textual basis here for the claim that discipleship is not open to all people. Christophe Singer has an interesting proposal. He contends that the terms of discipleship are intentionally put out of reach for everyone, since no one has sufficient devotion to fulfill Jesus' demands of absolute loyalty. The twin parables underscore that one has to take account of the inability to succeed on one's own resources. Only after recognition of this "defeat" can one be open to the application of divine mercy and empowerment, themes that will rise to the fore in Luke 15. Cf. "La difficulté d'être disciple: Luc 14/25–35,"

Exposition

Luke 14:26 ("anyone," τίς), Luke 14:27 ("whoever," ὅστις), as well as Luke 14:33 ("everyone/anyone," πᾶς).[100] The notion of inclusiveness will also extend to the parable of the Lost Sons, both of whom are the object of the father's affection.

THE PARABLES OF THE LOST (LUKE 15:1-32)

The lion's share of exegetical and theological reflection in the Lukan travel narrative centers on this chapter, and in particular the parable of the Lost Sons. The story continues to linger in the collective memory in many western societies, where it has inspired artistic creativity in both painting and literature.[101] Because of its literary position and its theological emphasis, Luke 15 has been called the "heart of the Third Gospel."[102] This *trio* of parables culminating in the popular story of the prodigal is above all revelatory of the heart of God and constitutes one of the most moving metaphors of divine love.

In the more limited literary context of Luke 14-16, the stories develop the themes of the preceding chapter. First, Luke 15 reaffirms Jesus' preoccupation with the marginalized and continues to trump the imagery of feasting (cf. Luke 14:1-24). The theme of reversal of fortune is also of paramount concern in this text, evident in an opulent cluster of inversion motifs, which remain to be discussed in detail. The concept of wisdom takes second stage by comparison, but Luke 15 makes a most significant contribution in linking it with repentance and so offers a vista of the subjective and psychological aspects of wisdom. Additional subtle nuances in characterization provide further augmentation of the sapiential deposits in Luke 14-16.

The historical prelude to the parables comes in the form of a scene that resumes the conflict, which we have encountered in Luke 14:1-6. The language of Luke 15:1-2 not only contrasts Jesus with the Pharisees and scribes, but also creates an antithesis between the latter group and the "sinners." The choice of aspect shows the behavior of the respective

21-36.

100. Green (*The Gospel of Luke*, 566) makes this point without explicitly connecting it to the parable of the Great Banquet.

101. For a detailed discussion on the parable's impact on literature and art, See Bovon, *Das Evangelium nach Lukas: Lk 15,1-,27*, 60-65.

102. Cf. Forbes, *The God of Old*, 109. Hendrickx (*The Parables of Jesus*, 138) makes the same point.

parties to be typical in that the predicate in Luke 15:1 (ἦσαν . . . ἐγγίζοντες) and the leading verb in Luke 15:2 (διεγόγγυζον) read as iterative imperfects.[103] The grumbling of the religious leaders was common enough. However, the verbal opposition also depicts a heightened intensity in conflict compared with the silence of Luke 14:4. In the context of mounting hostility, the following teachings surprise us with portraits of forgiveness and God's gracious action to save the lost,[104] a possibility also held out to the aggressors.

As has often been affirmed, the three stories ought to be read through the lens of Luke 15:1–2 and the contrasts set up in these introductory verses.[105] The parables of the Lost are Jesus' reply to the grumbling and rejection of the Pharisees, commending joy and reception of the repentant sinner instead. Beyond this, the two sons of the concluding story closely identify with the tax collectors and sinners as well as the scribes and Pharisees, respectively.

Although the parable of the Lost Sheep (Luke 15:4–7) also features in Matt 18:12–14,[106] Luke has joined all three stories together into a strongly unified text portion. The use of an overt *inclusio* of "lostness" and being found (ἀπόλλυμι/εὑρίσκω, Luke 15:4, 32) is only a small part of the text's cohesive fabric.

The Lost Sheep and the Lost Coin share particularly explicit structural qualities. The parallel patterning of this discourse pair evinces three main components for both stories, namely, narrative (the story of being lost and found: Luke 15:4–6a, 8–9a), a climactic utterance by the main character calling for rejoicing (Luke 15:6b, 9b), and a concluding "translation" of the story in terms of heavenly joy (Luke 15:7, 10). With such pronounced verbal and thematic affinities, the reader may be acutely tempted to conclude that the twin parables merely make the "same point."[107] Nonetheless, the transposition of the "lost" from the wilderness

---

103. The antithetical parallelism between the religious leaders and the despised is enhanced in several ways. First, there are phonetic correspondences in ἐγγίζοντες and διεγόγγυζον. Second, while one group draws near to "hear," the other distances itself from Jesus by "speaking" (λέγοντες). Finally, both parties consist of two sub-groups joined by the conjunctive καί.

104. Cf. Shellard, *New Light on Luke*, 118.

105. Cf. Just, *Luke 9:51—24:53*, 587; Green, *The Gospel of Luke*, 572.

106. Unlike Luke 15:7, Matthew's version of the Lost Sheep fails to state its theme as repentance. How Luke could identify repentance as the governing thought of the parable remains to be discussed.

107. So Shellard, *New Light on Luke*, 119.

to the domestic sphere is highly significant for our understanding of the triad of parables in Luke 15. With *people* being the ultimate referents of the twin parables of the Lost Sheep and the Lost Coin, the shift from "out there" to within suggests that one can be lost, not only in the wilderness of the big wide world, but also in the confines of one's own home. The contrast being one of space (or, location) is intended to prepare the reader for the final story of the triadic complex, in which *both* sons are lost: one far away from home, in the "wilderness," and the other so close to home, or rather, *in* the father's house.[108] The order in which the characters appear in their respective sphere of "lost-ness" iterates the movement of the two shorter parables and places both scenarios side by side. Both sons are lost, and both need to repent, but only the younger faces up to the challenge, or so it seems.[109]

An additional noteworthy variation between the first two tales warrants some comments. The parable of the Lost Coin features no contrast with the nine coins that are (presumably) accounted for, while the story of the Lost Sheep ends with a remarkable comparison of heavenly joy ("there will be *more* joy in heaven . . .," Luke 15:7). The omission in the second parable helps to intensify the focus on the call to communal joy. The call to rejoice is absolute. This emphasis sets the stage for the father's reaction to the son's return in the third story. He calls for grand celebrations in which the elder son refuses to participate. Joy is what is called for as the only appropriate response (notice ἔδει, Luke 15:32, "it was fitting"), and yet, joy is contrasted with the grumbling attitude of the elder son, who is a mirror image of the Pharisees and scribes in Luke 15:2 (διαγογγύζω).

The absence of the "righteous" in the parable of the Lost Coin may also help to link both the beginning and the ending of the chapter, where we encounter corresponding themes of moral impeccability. Read in this way, the reference to the righteous who need no repentance (Luke 15:7) is an ironic preview of the elder son's protest (Luke 15:29–30) which puts a premium on his own impeccability as opposed to the corruption of his "evil" brother.

---

108. The father's address to the elder son, "you are always with me" (σὺ πάντοτε μετ' ἐμοῦ εἶ, Luke 15:31) expresses the spatial proximity.

109. In this regard, it is worthwhile noting that Luke 15:11–32 deals from the beginning with a father of *two* sons: it is a two-pronged parable. Although a good deal of emphasis rests on the younger's homecoming, the second part of the story is integral to the whole. See Hendrickx, *The Parable of Jesus*, 150.

As Landmesser has noted, the numerical references also point to the third parable as the climax of the complex.[110] The loss of one sheep out of a herd of one hundred is considerable, but less grave than the loss of one drachma in a collection of ten. The loss of one son in Luke 15:11–32 is by far the greatest of all, it is a question of life and death (cf. Luke 15:24, 32). The triad of parables forms a trajectory aiming at the final story. The level of narrative detail and length of the parable confirms this, too.

This being the case, Luke invites the interpreter to read any one part of the chapter in light of the other two. The common elements of "lost," "found," and "joy" reinforce each other, while elements unique to only one (or two) part(s) of the trinity are complementary and may raise important questions because of their absence elsewhere.

Perhaps one of the most intriguing issues concerns the mention of "repentance" in the two introductory similes. The term ματάνοια is lacking in the parable of the Lost Sons, where repentance nevertheless forms a key theme of the plot. Read at face value, the same cannot be said about the shorter parables. Apart from Jesus' concluding comments (Luke 15:7, 10), these stories are not about repentance, but the considerable efforts at searching for what is lost. Repentance being a highly subjective idea, neither the sheep nor the coin can serve as illustrating the process. They are simply being found.[111] However, the verses only express a tension which had always been affirmed in Jewish concepts of repentance: A lost person cannot be found without repentance occurring.[112] This notion boasts a rich scriptural subtext, according to which human agency and divine sovereignty converge in causing a sinner to return to God (Deut 29:4; Deut 32:36; Ezek 34:11–16; Ps 23:1–4; 119:176).

The Lukan understanding of repentance is in this sense thoroughly informed by OT theology. He represents repentance as both an experience of "being found by a concerned seeker,"[113] as well as the product of human effort. However, Jesus' role as the seeker of the lost (cf. Luke 19:10) has primacy, without resulting in a portrait of strict divine determination

---

110. Landmesser, "Die Rückkehr ins Leben," 239–261, 245.

111. Many have argued the point that the comments of Luke 15:7, 10 are secondary, i.e., have been added by Luke. Cf. Broer, "Das Gleichnis vom verlorenen Sohn," 459; Fitzmyer, *The Gospel According to Luke X–XXIV*, 1073; Petzke, *Das Sondergut*, 138; Schottroff, "Das Gleichnis vom verlorenen Sohn," 32–35.

112. Cf. Bailey, *Poet and Peasant*, 155. Cf. also Wenham, *The Parables of Jesus*, 101.

113. Tannehill, *Luke*, 238.

in salvation.¹¹⁴ In this regard, the third parable is a necessary addition towards a fuller apprehension of repentance in Luke. The father loves his sons, waits and pleads with them, but his love can also be rejected. Repentance, while in essence theo-centric,¹¹⁵ remains subjective. The subjective aspect of repentance is highlighted in the younger son's soliloquy, and by the repetition of his personal confession (Luke 15:18–19, 21).¹¹⁶

Some exegetes argue that the younger son's motive is to be seen chiefly as a self-interested desire to avoid starvation and so hardly qualifies as true repentance.¹¹⁷ This verdict on the son's agenda assumes a dichotomy between suffering and repentance. Nonetheless, repentance may often be triggered by some form of deprivation. OT texts frequently show God using hardship to bring Israel to its senses (cf. Deut 30:1–2; Isa 1:5–6). In the case of the younger son, hunger stimulates repentance without necessarily casting a shadow of doubt on the genuineness of his remorse.¹¹⁸ Repentance does not occur in a historical vacuum.

The son's repentance, however, also connects with the wisdom motifs so far discussed in our study of Luke 14–16. The prodigal's selfishness eventually reduces him to the level of a hireling in a Gentile establishment. Famine and hunger complete the disaster, and the son's desperation is further indicated by his acceptance of a most abhorrent work for any religious Jew. The rabbinic adage, "None may rear pigs anywhere" (*m. B. Qam. 7.7*; cf. *b. B. Qam.* 82b), pronounces the cultic ban over the lad,¹¹⁹ whose food rations were so scanty that he even longed to eat the pigs' fodder.¹²⁰ By more or less common Jewish standards, the son has descended to the bottom of the social strata. He is covered with shame and has become a genuine outcast.

---

114. Stagg, "Luke's Theological," 227.

115. Cf. Landmesser, who speaks of μετάνοια as an act of forgiveness on the part of the father effecting a return to life ("Die Rückkehr," 257).

116. Pokorny, *Theologie*, 165. A similar conclusion is reached in Sterling, "Turning to God," Gray and O'Day, *Scripture and Traditions*, 69–95.

117. So Bailey, *Finding the Lost*, 129–33; Hoppe, "Gleichnis und Situation," 4–5.

118. Forbes, *God of Old*, 136.

119. Pigs, of course, were unclean animals under levitical legislation (Lev 11:7; cf. Deut 14:8). The son's constant involvement with the animals would have rendered him unfit for any cultic performance and put him into a religious nowhere-land, outside of traditional Jewish life and practice.

120. This detail may suggest that he had sunk even below the status of an unclean animal. Cf. Bock, *Luke 9:51—24:53*, 1313.

In his soliloquy (Luke 15:17–19), the younger son surveys his woes and decides to return to his father's house. He fully acknowledges his sin before God (εἰς τὸν οὐρανὸν, Luke 15:18) and man (father). Although he still holds the status of "son" by birth, he is prepared to enter his father's house as a hired servant (μίσθος, Luke 15:19). A μίσθος was hired for one day at a time. On a landowner's property, he was less cared for than a slave (δοῦλος), since the latter remained a constant part of the clan. Far from acting out of selfish motives (as he used to),[121] the son knows he is at the mercy of his father. He humbles himself and in assigning to himself the most inferior position in the patriarchal establishment, the younger son fulfills the protasis of the second part of the wisdom saying of Luke 14:11.[122] He takes the "lowest seat" (cf. Luke 14:10). And because he humbles himself, he will also be exalted. Just as pride implies humiliation, so "humility comes before honor" (Prov 15:33; Prov 18:12; Prov 29:23). The young man is thus also one who acknowledges his folly in order to apply his heart to wisdom (cf. Prov 1:4, 20–23).

The turning point of the lad's fortunes arrives when he acknowledges his sin before "heaven" (and father), an idiomatic expression for his repentant attitude before God (cf. Exod 10:16; 1 Sam 7:6; Tob. 3:3; Jdt. 5:17). Wisdom's guiding principle, the fear of Yahweh being the *beginning* of wisdom (Prov 1:7; Prov 9:10), may be seen in the "Erkenntnisszene"[123] ("scene of perception") culminating in the son's soliloquy (Luke 15:17–19), which defines the beginning of his journey homewards.

His humility is further pronounced in his professed personal *worth* (ἄξιος, Luke 15:19). Worth implies comparison and is intrinsic, irrespective of one's position in the social hierarchy. In other words, the son is not

---

121. *Pace* Bailey (*Poet and Peasant*, 176–78), who argues that his proposal is rather business-like and opens the door to a future restoration in status. Accordingly, Bailey (*Finding the Lost*, 133–35) reads the particle οὐκέτι (Luke 15:19a) as "not at the present time." The meaning "no longer" or "not anymore," however, is to be preferred. The contrast in the son's confession of sin lies in what he used to be and his present situation. The two scenarios (son vs. hired servant) are in this sense exclusive of each other. Either he is a son or a servant, and if he is now a servant, he can no longer be a son. A possible reinstatement in the future introduces a scenario that destroys the logic of the son's words and adds an element that is not grounded textually.

122. The younger son arguably fills both principles stated in Luke 14:11. As a careless and proud fellow, he is humiliated. When he truly humbles himself before his father, he is exalted.

123. Cf. Eckey, *Das Lukasevangelium 11:1—24:53*, 688.

Exposition

only accepting a *position* below sonship, but he *sees* himself as being of less personal valuation than his brother.

The father's repeated analogy of the younger son's repentance as a revival (Luke 15:24, 32) affords another connection with traditional wisdom themes. The rationale for the invitation to the party (i.e., the return to life, being found) occurs at a point in the tale where the first two parables speak of repentance.[124] A comparison with the shorter stories in chapter 15 thus reveals that repentance is portrayed as a return to life. The deliberate choice of wisdom over folly as a return to life is a bedrock motif of Jewish sapiential tradition, too.

Prov 14:27 is representative of a number of texts that suggest a movement parallel to the father's analogy: "The fear of Yahweh is a fountain of life, that one may turn from the snares of death" (cf. also Prov 4:4, 13, 22–23; Prov 13:14; LXX 22:4; LXX 24:9). The language of Prov 8:35–36 is perhaps even more explicit: "Whoever finds me [wisdom] finds life and obtains favor from Yahweh, but he who fails to find me injures himself; all who hate me love death." In classic Jewish wisdom literature, the life of sin is death, whereas finding wisdom is a return to life, sometimes even likened to the most pristine quality of a "tree of life" (Prov 3:18; Prov 11:30).[125] In his journey back to his father's home, the son discovers the path of wisdom leading to life (Prov 19:23).

The son's life prior to making an about face evinces a number of thought-provoking details that would also warrant consideration of traditional wisdom themes. In short, the selfish lad acts like the proverbial rebellious fool.[126] The wayward son bringing dishonor to his parents is a staple feature of wisdom instruction (Prov 10:5; Prov 17:2; Prov 19:26; Prov 28:24; Prov 29:15; LXX 20:9a; Sir. 22:3). In particular, the references to "squandering" (διασκορπίζω) and "extravagant lifestyle" (ζῶν ἀσώτως, Luke 15:13) may make the reader think of the foolish son who refuses instruction. The indulgent life of a rebellious son which shames the parents is described in LXX Prov 28:7 as ἀσωτία. Although the cognate noun (ἀσωτία) does not appear in LXX Prov 23:31, this text sketches the same concept of wasteful and ruinous living resulting in the shame of

---

124. Landmesser ("Die Rückkehr," 256–57) makes this interesting point: "Μετάνοια ist die vom Vater, von dem das Leben neu schaffenden Schöpfer, im Akt der Vergebung bewirkte *Rückkehr in das Leben*."

125. For an analysis of the use of the phrase "tree of life" in Proverbs, see Fields, "Proverbs 11:30," 517–35.

126. Cf. Pöhlmann, *Der verlorene Sohn*, 183–85.

the family. TestJud. 14:1–5 (second century B.C.) develops an even more inclusive portrait of the son as drunkard who associates with prostitutes and dubious characters.

The elder son's depreciable comments about his brother (Luke 15:30) are also suggestive of the typical fool in wisdom literature.[127] The reference to his brother's involvement with prostitutes echoes the wealth of sapiential instruction warning against the seductress who takes advantage of the fool (cf. Prov 7:5–23; Prov 9:13–18). Significantly, those who fall for her end up in the house of the living dead (Prov 7:23; Prov 9:18), somewhat reminiscent of the father's summary of his younger son's former life of dissipation (Luke 15:24, 32). His brother's sketch appears to set him up as the antitype of the wise son depicted in Prov 29:3: "He who loves wisdom makes his father glad, but a companion of prostitutes squanders his wealth" (cf. Ben Sirach 9:6). In light of the texts adduced so far, the characterization of the prodigal son seems to own stronger links to the proverbial fool of Israel's wisdom tradition than to the cited rebellious son of Deut 21:18–21, who is described as "a glutton and a drunkard" (Deut 21:20).[128]

The elder son's self-portrait, on the other hand, would fit the bill of the wise son of Prov 28:7a, who never transgresses the father's commandment (cf. Luke 15:29). But, of course, his view of his own moral impeccability is inflated, and he is far from the ideal of the model son that he makes himself out to be. His treatment of his father, who now "goes out" (Luke 15:28) to one of his sons a second time in the story, is nothing short of an insult. The son's refusal to join the festivities heaps public shame on the father,[129] and parallels the affront of the cheap excuses in the parable

---

127. It is not clear as to whether the comments of Luke 15:30 are to be seen as based on credible information. Given the hostile attitude of the elder brother, his words could just as well be contemptuous speculation, aiming at presenting the brother in the worst possible light. The reference to prostitutes in Luke 15:30 certainly connects with Luke's historical setting (Luke 15:1–2), in which scribes and Pharisees complain about "sinners." Cf. Stein, *Luke*, 408.

128. The list of commentators who draw attention to Deut 21:18–21 includes (among others) Bailey, *Finding the Lost*, 122–24; Forbes (referring to Bailey), *God of Old*, 143; Bock, *Luke 9:51—24:53*, 1319; Shellard, *New Light on Luke*, 119; Pokorny, *Theologie der lukanischen Schriften*, 167.

129. Bailey (*Finding the Lost*, 172) describes in detail how the son's resentment against his father would have warranted severe punishment in a first century Middle Eastern setting.

Exposition

of the Great Banquet.¹³⁰ The lack of a title in the son's address to the father (cf. Luke 15:29) also qualifies as a sign of contempt. He accuses his father of favoritism (Luke 15:29–30) and professes that he does not belong to the family (Luke 15:30). Indeed, the elder's words contain the complaint that he is unable to dispose of his share of the property (cf. Luke 15:29). Perhaps he too entertained a death wish for his father.

In due consideration of the elder son's troubled relationship with both his father and younger brother, he turns out to be a character who exalts himself in the sense of the maxim of Luke 14:11. If he does not change, his humiliation seems inevitable (cf. Prov 29:23; Prov 8:13; LXX 28:26). Prov 30:11–14 provides a rather felicitous survey of his heart's landscape: "There are those who curse their fathers and do not bless their mothers. There are those who are clean in their own eyes but are not washed from their filth. There are those—how lofty are their eyes, how high their eyelids lift! There are those whose teeth are swords, whose fangs are knives, to devour the poor from off the earth, the needy from among mankind."

The father's role in the tale is perhaps more difficult to read in terms of wisdom themes. However, it is curious that apart from a passing reference in Tob. 8:21 the specific and absurd idea of granting an inheritance while alive is discussed only in Sir. 33:19–23, one of Israel's books of wisdom. As Witherington has demonstrated, some of Jesus' teachings evoke a memory of Ben Sirach.¹³¹ Could this shocking narrative detail be another instance incorporating teachings from this popular literary work? This would mean that the father's highly irregular behavior is specifically geared towards *defying* (and in this sense *correcting*) traditional wisdom thought, indeed, the father violates a whole list of conventions. He becomes an oddball by ancient Jewish standards.

Besides the shock of his initial grant to the younger son, when he would be expected to refuse the audacious demand (Sir. 33:19–23), Talbert also cites the amazing reaction to the proposal of receiving the prodigal as a day laborer (Luke 15:19).¹³² "A typical Jewish father might have considered this expedient until the son's reformation had been confirmed. It would, moreover, allow the youth to make reparations required

---

130. Cf. Wolter, "LK 15 als Streitgespräch," 46. Wolter draws the connection to the Banquet (Luke 14:16–24) and links the elder son with the νομικοί of 11:52. Like the son, they refuse to "enter" (εἰσέρχομαι).

131. Cf. Witherington, *Jesus the Sage*, 205–8.

132. Talbert, *Reading Luke*, 179–80.

by repentance (cf. Luke 19:8). Instead, the father came out of the house and in a dramatic demonstration showed an unexpected love publicly, even to the point of humiliating himself."[133] Once again, it is the sage Ben Sirach who informs us that it was considered beneath the dignity of an older man to run in public (Sir. 19:30).

The excessive joy of the father is as puzzling as the extravagance of the ensuing festivities. But this appears to be the crux of the story: unlike the behavior of the sons, the love of the father cannot be captured in sapiential traditions. It is so extraordinary that it explodes the categories of wisdom and may even seem foolish by some such inherited standards. Although the father's professed rationale for the excessive joy pleads for appropriateness (ἔδει, Luke 15:32), the father's wisdom is also foolishness—at least in the eyes of one of his sons.[134] The story is thus a beautiful and stunning revelation of the loving heart of God placed squarely at the center not only of chapters 14–16, but the entire Lukan gospel.

The parables of the Lost feature an array of reversal motifs. The repetitious vocabulary of the first two shorter stories in itself spells out the change from "being lost" (ἀπόλλυμι, Luke 15:4 [2x], 8, 9) to "being found" (εὑρίσκω, Luke 15:4, 5, 6, 9 [2x]).[135] This inversion is then expounded in terms of a sinner's repentance (Luke 15:7, 10), although the two stories offer no hint whatsoever at the psychological aspects of repentance. It is not until the younger son's return to his father's house in the third story that this image comes into view.

Feasting and joy are also pronounced in the two opening parables. Although the natural semantic opposition, namely mourning, is absent from the text, the process of seeking what is lost is hardly a joyful occasion. Instead, both shepherd and woman conduct a diligent search (cf. Luke 15:8) intended not only to signify the relative worth of the lost goods, but the measure of anxiety that informs the search. The extravagant joy of having found what was lost underscores the impression that the stories describe a movement from concern or anxiety to joy. This in turn has profound implications for God's emotional investment in the matter of repentance, as the sayings of Luke 15:7, 10 reveal. Divine exuberant joy over the return of a sinner is finally pictured in the concrete example of

133. Ibid., 180.

134. Paul's oxymoron about the "foolishness of God" may come to mind (cf. 1 Cor 1:18–25).

135. The same reversal (lost/found) drives the closing words of the third parable (Luke 15:32) and therefore brings literary unity to the three stories.

Exposition

the father's reception of his lost son. The twin reversal of "lost/found" and "anxiety/rejoicing" provides the super-structure for the entire chapter.[136]

The prodigal son's tale throws into relief several pertinent themes of inversion. Viewed against the backdrop of the adage of Luke 14:11, he undergoes the full sweep of changes resulting in transposition. By acting proudly and without concern for others, he sets himself up for a fall. Conversely, by humbling himself he experiences exaltation and reinstatement in the father's household. The younger son thus fulfills the movements of the saying from Luke 14:11 as well as the corresponding paradigm of Luke 1:51–52 in the Magnificat (for the reversal described in Luke 1:53 see below).

Similarly, the prodigal experiences a change from shame to honor, which also closely aligns with both Luke 14:7–11 and 1:51–52. The son had broken the rules and conventions of his society by asking his father for his share of the inheritance in order to take off to a distant place. He initiated "a breakdown of the solidarity of the family,"[137] to say the least. K. H. Rengstorf argues that the prodigal's selfish behavior would have resulted in the ceremonial cutting off of the son from the community (a so-called *ketsatsah*).[138] It is not entirely clear what kind of transaction was required for the *ketsatsah*, whether one had to sell to Gentiles (cf. *Ruth Rab.* 7:11; *Kidd.* 1:5) or merely to an outsider (cf. *Ket.* 2:10). The text certainly offers no suggestion that we are to assume the ceremony was in fact performed, but, as Bock rightly claims,[139] Rengstorf's study affords us appreciable access to the social context of the original audience and indicates the kind of emotions which would arise in a patriarchal first century Palestinian community. The son's descent into public shame is complete with the arrival of the famine, leading to the desperate move of caring for pigs, which are "repugnant to Jewish sensibilities."[140]

---

136. Marshall (*The Gospel of Luke*, 597) conveniently summarizes the theme of the three parables as the "joy which is experienced by a person who recovers what he has lost."

137. Cf. Nolland, *Luke 9:21—18:34*, 789.

138. Rengstorf, *Die Re-Investitur des verlorenen Sohnes*. Bailey (*Finding the Lost*, 121) concurs in concluding that "If the *qetsatsah* ceremony was not enacted when he left, surely it will be performed if he dare return under these latter unthinkable circumstances."

139. Bock, *Luke 9:51—24:53*, 1310n10.

140. Nolland, *Luke 9:21—18:34*, 789.

The prodigal's shame is turned on its head through the father's promotion from his professed servile status (Luke 15:19, 21) to the extravagant reception and re-instatement as son. The father makes sure that the whole village takes note of his son's return to his former position through several public insignia bestowed upon the son, culminating in the great feast held in honor of the returnee.[141]

But the younger son's experience also illustrates the Magnificat's second main reversal (Luke 1:53). "No one gave him anything," (Luke 15:16) describes the lost son at his lowest point in the narrative, plagued by hunger. The village party set up by his overjoyed father signals a radical change in the son's fortunes. The hungry are indeed filled "with good things" (Luke 1:53).

A very closely related theme of reversal portrayed in the text centers on the contrast "isolation/separation" vs. "inclusion/integration." Loneliness and isolation are already implied in the son's distance from home, but become explicit in the above-cited words, "No one gave him anything." The prodigal is left to himself and on his own in his misery. As an outcast, he cannot expect help from anyone. However, his return to the father's house does not only lead to a restored relationship with the gracious father, but he is re-integrated into both family and village community.[142] "There is shalom between the prodigal and the family,"[143] precisely the notion resented by the older brother. Along with reconciliation, sorrow is turned into joy, which resonates with the conclusions of the two preceding parables.[144] The same is true for the concluding words of the father employing the pairing of "lost" and "found" already known from Luke 15:1–10.

The elder son's bitter words imply a situation, which compares with one aspect of his brother's return in a striking way. For just as the prodigal took the "lowest seat" by offering his father his hand as a hireling,

141. Cf. Marshall, *The Gospel of Luke*, 610–11.

142. Cf. Eckey, *Das Lukasevangelium II, 11:1—24:53*, 691.

143. Bailey, *Finding the Lost*, 169. Bailey follows von Rad in reading the reference to the son's return in "sound" condition (Luke 15:27, ὑγιαίνω) as heavily freighted with the use of the word in the LXX, where it almost invariably translates the Hebrew word *shalom*. In this sense, the "health report" of Luke 15:27 cannot be limited to the son's physical condition (which would have been rather poor, considering his prior circumstances). Luke 15:27 can be read as saying, "Your father extended his *shalom* to your brother."

144. This reversal theme is stated categorically in the beatitudes of Luke's Sermon on the Plain (Luke 6:21b).

his brother also sees himself as less than a rightful son. His claim is to have worked like a slave for the father (cf. Luke 15:29, δουλεύω), a detail reminiscent of the younger's self-abasement. In the older son's case, the words are a volley directed against the father, as the list of complaints in Luke 15:29 shows. The younger's offer to work as a hired servant, on the other hand, connects with his personal worth ("I am no longer worthy to be called your son," Luke 15:19). He puts the blame on himself. Nonetheless, the older brother's innuendo of having slaved for his father implies a demotion, and in this sense on ironic reversal, too. His relationship with the father is strained, and his words tend to put a distance between father and himself. Perhaps it is significant that both sons are said to have come home from the "field" (ἀγρός, cf. Luke 15:15, 25), intimating that both start out some distance away from the father's house, even though the older never really left the homestead. But in the context of the parable, this detail could mean that both were lost. So far as the story goes, therefore, the older son gives no indication that the personal distance has been overcome. The needed reversal does not materialize because he does not come home. In his words the reader hears the views of the "ninety-nine righteous who need no repentance" (Luke 15:7; cf. also Luke 15:29: ". . . never disobeyed your command"). Given the fact that the parable is Jesus' response to the Pharisees' grumbling, and based on the rule of end stress,[145] the elder son's interaction with the father is the story's climax.

As for the father, he remains consistent in all his dealings throughout the story. If he was generous at the beginning in giving the son his wish, he outdoes himself by re-integrating him, and no questions asked. Likewise, in his responses to his sons he does not seem to be concerned with the restoration of his own damaged honor.[146] The younger is received with a kiss, and the father is not outraged by the older son's refusal to participate in the festivities, nor does he react in anger over the son's disrespectful words to him. He demonstrates love to both sons by coming out to meet them. The parable thus highlights the love of God as being inclusive. It is extended to the repentant as well as the hardened. In light of this, Stein suggests that the parable should be named after the main character in both halves of the parables, namely, "the parable of the gracious father."[147]

145. The rule simply states that a parable's climax comes at the end. Cf. Stein, *Luke*, 402.
146. Cf. Tannehill, *Luke*, 241.
147. Stein, *Luke*, 402.

THE DISHONEST MANAGER (LUKE 16:1–13)

As the sustained focus on economic matters intimates, the emphasis in Luke 16 rests on the Magnificat's second theme of reversal (Luke 1:53). In accord with the carefully balanced presentation of the material, Jesus' words now appeal to the disciples, before Luke 16:14–31 rounds off chapters 14–16 with material primarily addressed to the opposition.[148]

The relationship of Luke 16:1–13 to the parables of the Lost has been a question on which no consensus has been reached. Some interpreters have been content in arguing that there is no specific connection to be found after all, or that the issue remains unclear.[149] Others conceded a loose relationship between the two text units, based upon the repetition of the word διασκορπίζω (Luke 15:13; Luke 16:1).[150] Preisker took his cue from this textual detail and concluded that the Parable of the Dishonest Manager gives the contrast to the prodigal who, after squandering his wealth, repented.[151]

Preisker's case is unconvincing. Even if Luke 16:8 is judged not to be part of the parable (as Preisker does),[152] the following remark about the "unjust steward" indicates that the steward's behavior was meant to be a *positive* example for the disciples, the nature and limits of which remain to be probed. The point of this story is hardly an "awful warning" against the powers of demonic greed, even though Jesus' addendum (Luke 16:9–13) includes such a warning. The steward's lack of repentance is irrelevant to the parable and does not afford a valid point of comparison with the prodigal son.

Bailey suggests that the link between Luke 15:11–32 and Luke 16:1–8 is mercy,[153] drawing a parallel between the merciful father of Luke 15:11–32 and the "merciful" lord from the Dishonest Manager. The pur-

---

148. The reader may recall the discussion of chapter 2 of this study under "Internal Textual Coherence" (2.2.). One of the defining characteristics of Luke 14–16 is the way that Jesus addresses his antagonists and disciples in a consistently alternating pattern.

149. So Shellard, *New Light on Luke*, 120; Stein, *Luke*, 411; Petzke, *Das Sondergut*, 143; Ringe, *Luke*, 212.

150. Fitzmyer, *The Gospel According to Luke X–XXIV*, 1095; Gooding, *According to Luke*, 272.

151. Preisker, "Lukas 16, 1–7," 85–92.

152. According to the majority of commentators (cf. the discussion of Landry and May, "Honor Restored," 288–89), the parable ends in Luke 16:8a, with Luke 16:8bff. forming Jesus' commentary. This study adopts this view.

153. Bailey, *Poet and Peasant*, 86–110.

pose of both parables, then, is to reveal the mercy of God. The steward, so Bailey, trusted the character of his lord (known in the community as a "generous and merciful"[154] man) and staked everything on this his master's trait, assuming he would let his less than honest adjustments stand.

I find it difficult to obtain Bailey's notion of a "merciful lord" from the story, and the parable's purpose is surely not to reveal God's mercy. The crucial point of the story hinges on "shrewdness" (ὅτι φρονίμως ἐποίμσεν, Luke 16:8), rather than mercy. Moreover, the reader is not to learn from the *master's* behavior as the catalyst for Jesus' teachings on discipleship, but it is the steward whose savvy measures become an object lesson for Jesus' followers. The interpretive comment regarding being received into "eternal dwellings" in Luke 16:9 certainly indicates that the parable is concerned with eschatology,[155] but the eschatological nuance does not rest on some character trait of the master. It is merely the steward's crisis and his use of (worldly) wisdom that translates into an eschatological metaphor. For the said reasons, Bailey's idea of an implicit thematic congruence between the two stories appears to be unlikely.

In a brief article entitled "The Hypocritical Son," M. R. Austin argued that the two parables form a pair on different grounds.[156] Taking his cue from a comparison of the prodigal son and the unjust steward, Austin notes that both stories begin with a reference to "squandering" property belonging to another. In each story, a turning point is reached when the main character faces a crisis and has a moment of self-awareness (cf. Luke 15:17; Luke 16:3).[157] Again, in each case, the protagonist acts from motives of self-interest.[158] The stories close with the main character being received. A very similar argument, based on selfish motives as a point of comparison, was later made by Kilgallen.[159]

Austin's analysis points up a number of interesting parallels, but also has its weakness. A crucial question arises from the notion of cool calculation attributed to the son's reaction to the crisis. To be fair, Austin

---

154. Ibid., 102.
155. Ibid., 107.
156. Austin, "The Hypocritical Son," 307–15.
157. Ibid., 311.
158. Ibid., 311–12.
159. Kilgallen, "Luke 15 and 16," 369–76. Kilgallen characterizes the prodigal's sentiments with the words: "Clever young man, indeed!" (373). The selfish ambition of the son is then placed side by side with the trickster's duping of his master in Luke 16:1–8.

himself anticipates this object by conceding that the son's selfish ambition was modified by other motives, too. He even admits the possibility that the son actually *was* penitent.[160] Whether or not his repentance was totally selfless is surely besides the point, but the fact is that when read in conjunction with the two shorter introductory stories (Luke 15:1–10), the prodigal's return to his father's home pictures a repentant sinner (Luke 15:7, 10). To speak of self-interest on his part is merely to highlight how the youngster's circumstances facilitated repentance. Hardship leading God's people to repentance is a well-known theme from the OT, in that Yahweh's punishments of Israel (famine, sword, pestilence) always aimed at bringing the people to their senses (cf. Deut 28:1–68; Deut 30:1–6; 2 Chr 20:9). In the world of the OT, suffering becomes an incentive to seek the Lord. In a similar way, the prodigal's return does not spell a case study in cackling cleverness, but the tale is about the son's brokenness which finds verbal expression in his confession(s) (cf. Luke 15:18–19, 21). He pictures a penitent sinner who has finally run out of steam. So his return to the father's οἶκος symbolizes a sinner's return to God.

In advancing his case, I believe Austin has missed a great opportunity. He rightly lists the notable parallels that connect the stories at a structural level. The numerous points of comparison may be shown as follows:

Prodigal Son (Luke 15:11–32)	Unjust Steward (Luke 16:1–8)
Selfish character (vs. 12–13)	Unreliable character (vs. 1)
Squanders father's resources (vs. 13b)	Squanders master's resources (vs. 1)
Crisis: Hunger (vs. 14–17)	Crisis: Homeless (vs. 3–4)
Soliloquy (vs. 17–19)	Soliloquy (vs. 3–4)
Risk: At father's mercy (vs. 18–19)	Risk: Debtor' reciprocation (vs. 4–7)
Surprise: Father's reception (vs. 20–24)	Surprise: Master's commendation (vs. 8a)

The plot of both stories builds up to a crisis, which triggers the main character's monologue surveying the situation and (in the case of the prodigal son) spelling out the course of action. On an abstract level, both son and steward make a choice that implies some risk in that it leaves them at the mercy of someone else. Even though the manager is able to gain some leverage with the master's debtors, the anticipated outcome of being received into their houses (cf. Luke 16:4b) remains a matter beyond

---

160. Austin, "The Hypocritical Son," 311–12.

Exposition

his control. The surprise element in both parables comes at the end of the story, with the father's marvelously extravagant reception and the lord's most unexpected commendation. The structural affinities between the two parables are thus firmly established. The question remains as to what we are to conclude from the parallelism.

That the story of the prodigal is one about repentance as well as the unconditional love of the father is beyond dispute. In light of the above parallels, nothing would be easier than to posit a similar scenario for the Dishonest Manager, namely to focus not only on the manager, but to develop the lord's character, too. Accordingly, the master's disposition has been called "honorable"[161] and "merciful,"[162] attributes, which are hard to support from the text. The master's character may be the object of speculation, but Jesus' story remains very stingy in providing us with concrete information about the man's agenda. All we know is that he intends to fire an unreliable steward. Shall we infer from this that he has a sense of justice or a reasonable comprehension of proper work ethics? To be sure, the lord is indispensable in the story, but his character is otherwise undeveloped. This would lead me to suggest that his role is inherently *functional*, that is his words of rebuke constitute the crisis situation, and his commendation furnishes the surprise effect of the story. With this, the lord's role has fulfilled its purpose, and the main focal point is squarely on how the steward navigates the crisis.

This notion is the key to a more promising comparison between the two stories. At the level of the father and the master the affinities are more formal in nature, but in the case of the son and the manager the parallels also include psychological nuances. After all, the manager is commended for his use of wisdom, and the son, as we have argued at length, is a character who mirrors the reversal stated in Luke 14:11. His wisdom is to humble himself before father and God, to place himself at his father's mercy, and he is exalted. Using wisdom as a perspective on both stories, we may say that two complementary features crystallize. On the one hand, wisdom implies humility (or, being humbled), on the other, wisdom has a calculating aspect to it: What does it take to succeed? The story of the manager thus shows a similar concern as the previous instruction on discipleship with its call to count the costs (Luke 14:25–35), except that the parable of the Dishonest Manager is more overtly eschatological.

---

161. Cf. Just, *Luke 9:51—24:53*, 614: ". . . the lord is an honorable man."

162. Bailey, *Poet and Peasant*, 98.

The question remains as to how exactly we are to construe the manager's action in reducing the debts. In light of the fact that the comment of Luke 16:8a calls him "dishonest" (ἀδικία) only after the transactions described in Luke 16:5–7 makes the possibility of interpreting his actions as moral highly unlikely.[163] The initial charge of "squandering" (Luke 16:1) shows the steward as inept or incompetent, but not necessarily "unjust." The charge of ἀδικία is best explained with a view to his high-handed fixing of the accounts.

Still, it has been suggested that the steward was acting righteously by excluding the interest that had been figured into the amounts owed to the master,[164] or by reducing the debt due by the amount of his own commission.[165] Based upon the Greco-Roman patronage society, the debt reduction also produced the side effect of not only pleasing the debtors but also putting the master in a good light (i.e., restoring his *honor*).[166] Such readings of the parable take their cue from the fact that the master praised the steward for his conduct. How could he do this, unless his measures precipitated some form of advantage for the master? Nonetheless, the parable itself does not at all suggest any concern for the master's honor, and it is doubtful, to say the least, that Jesus (or Luke) could have expected the hearers (readers) to entertain such a prerequisite understanding.[167] Even if the exacting of unlawful interests was common practice among Palestinian Jews,[168] this interpretation assumes a profound

---

163. Cf. Stein, *Luke*, 412.

164. Donahue, *The Gospel in Parable*, 164; Derrett, *Law in the New Testament*, 72–77.

165. Fitzmyer, *The Gospel According to Luke X–XXIV*, 1098.

166. Cf. Kloppenborg, "The Dishonored Master," 475–92; Landry and May, "Honor Restored," 287–309.

167. A point well argued by Greene, "The Parable of the Unjust Steward," 82–89. "The issue of threatened honor may be on the periphery, but it certainly is not the explicit focus of the stated text" (84). Greene also raises the question of why the appended interpretation in Luke 16:8b-13 does not show any concern for the master's honor, if indeed this was a main factor in the story.

168. Cf. Bindemann, "Ungerechte als Vorbilder?" 955–70. Bindemann sees the steward's actions as a fulfillment of the "Geist" of the Torah, according to which interest was not to be exacted from fellow Jews. Says Bindemann: "Ungerechte können sich auf den Weg der Gerechtigkeit begeben und werden damit zur lebendigen Frage an herrschende Moral!" (967). In other words, the unjust steward becomes a model of righteous conduct posing a challenge for societal conventions. This in turn also made the master look better than he was. Bindemann fails to explain why the steward should then still be called "unjust." He also ignores the fact that the master's

change of agenda on the part of the landowner. But the story refuses to explain why a man who used to have no scruples about charging interests (assuming this to have been the case for the sake of the argument) should now be more concerned about his honor as an upstanding citizen.

It is also fair to remind us of the fact that the manager's preoccupation with restoring or increasing his master's honor is speculative at best, but his selfish ambition is not. After all, he is not commended for restoring his master's reputation in the community, but the reason cited by the master is that he acted with foresight in preparing for his *own* future.[169] And if, as I argued above, the role of the master is seen in more functional terms, the comment of Luke 16:8a does not require explanations that are extraneous to the parable. It is neither dishonesty nor acting righteously that furnishes the grounds for the commendation; it is merely the shrewd maneuvering and rising to the challenge of the man who finds himself in an existential crisis. This challenge involving the risk of losing status and resources suggests a scenario that, as Greene points out, "need not be tied exclusively to specific cultural boundaries."[170]

This recognition also helps to throw into sharper relief the transformation that the steward undergoes in the story. He used to be (or at least seemed to be) an incompetent administrator whose ineptness causes him to lose his managerial position. With his audacious fixing of the accounts, however, he has shown (perhaps unexpected) resourcefulness and so avoided certain economic disaster for himself. Similarly, the prodigal son's pride and selfishness are turned on their head by his humble return to his father's home. He could have been written off (he was lost), but he came back.

The conclusion that the steward cheated his master by falsifying the records of debts harmonizes with the closing comments of Jesus (Luke 16:8b–13). First, the steward's express purpose is that "people may receive me into their houses" (Luke 16:4). He anticipates that his scheming will ingratiate the debtors toward him so as to secure his future reception.[171] Jesus' application of the steward's selfish plots to the interests of the disciples shows a parallel logic. They are to "make friends" by using wealth, so that in the end "they may receive you into the eternal dwell-

---

commendation does not concern itself with Torah-righteousness, but only with the manager's shrewdness.

169. Cf. Marshall, *The Gospel of Luke*, 614.
170. Greene, "The Parable of the Unjust Steward," 87.
171. Cf. Stein, *Luke*, 413.

ings" (Luke 16:9). If the disciples' interest in the heavenly kingdom is uncompromised, they will use money or goods "faithfully" (Luke 16:10), namely in accord with God's will. The attribute of faithfulness thus stands in sharp contrast with the "injustice" (ἀδικία) of the steward who acts in accord with his own ends.

By holding out the promise of being received into eternal dwellings, a metaphor for the kingdom of God, Jesus also reinterprets the crisis of the manager in terms of an eschatological crisis for the disciples.[172] The looming crisis of judgment must be navigated through the wise use of wealth—not by giving away someone else's means, but by being generous with one's own. A disciple responds to the future crisis by a detachment from wealth.[173] Wisdom thus translates into foresight and taking appropriate measures for oneself, which is the common ground between the steward and the disciple of Jesus. However, as Luke 16:10–13 shows, the end does not justify unjust means. It is, after all, not the leverage that one can get with one's neighbor that ensures reception, but it is the verdict of God based on a life of commitment to the ethics of the heavenly kingdom. In this sense, the main character of the parable is also a model one must avoid.[174]

The specific act of reducing a debtor's burden also appears to have been considered a virtue of wisdom. Although the steward does this in an unlawful way, his "solution" to the crisis conforms in some ways to the didactic injunctions of liberality and generosity known from wisdom literature (cf. Prov 11:24–25; Prov 15:27; Prov 19:6, 17; Prov 21:25–26; Prov 28:8, 27; Prov 29:7; cf. also Ps 37:25–26). The cancellation of debt too lies at the heart of the sabbatical year and the Jubilee (Lev 25:8–17; Deut 15:1–6). Morschauser[175] cites an interesting wisdom teaching from the *Instruction of Amenemope* (26.14), which bears mentioning at this point. It renders advice to the administration scribes and managers such as the one in the parable. The text indicates that the lessening of financial burdens constituted an application of wisdom:

> If you find a large debt against a private citizen: Make it into three parts, forgive two, let one stand: You will find it a path of life. After sleep, when you wake in the morning, you will find it

---

172. Cf. Ireland, *Stewardship*, 214–15.
173. Forbes, *God of Old*, 178.
174. Ibid., 178.
175. Morschauser, "Revolution Economics?" 51–52.

good news. Better is praise with the love of men, than wealth in the storehouse. Better is bread with a happy heart, than wealth with vexation . . . God prefers him who honors the one in need, to him who worships the wealthy . . .

The forgiveness of debts as well as the resulting "social harmony and enhancement of one's personal reputation"[176] are themes strikingly reminiscent of the parable of the Dishonest Manager. Notwithstanding his misappropriating of the master's goods, the reduction of debts can be related to Israel's wisdom literature and, more generally, to time-honored values upheld throughout the ancient Mediterranean world. In this sense, Jesus' use of an "unjust" character as a trajectory for his wisdom instructions to the disciples becomes even more plausible.

Another aspect of Jesus' commentary is noteworthy. In speaking of one's relationship to money (wealth, Luke 16:11), the disciple is to think of himself as a steward who is required to be "faithful" (cf. Luke 16:10, 11, 12). However the disciple uses wealth, it is ultimately not his own, but the Lord's. Hence the words, "And if you have not been faithful in that which is another's, who will give you that which is your own?" (Luke 16:12). Jesus' analogy rests on the dichotomy between what one has but does not own (temporal goods, money) and that which truly belongs to the disciple. The latter notion has previously been described as "the true riches" (Luke 16:11). In dealing with temporal wealth, therefore, the disciple faces an ironic situation that reminds us of the unjust steward: It is only through the use of means that belong to the Lord that one can expect to be commended. But unlike the parable's main character, the disciple's use of the Lord's wealth requires a new attitude to material wealth that spells accountability rooted in love for the Lord (Luke 16:13). In a real sense, the disciple is to see himself as a "have-not" until being given what is forever one's own in the kingdom of God. Jesus' disciples—whatever their economic status—are the "blessed poor" of this world (cf. Luke 4:18; Luke 6:20). His words hint at a reversal that prepares us for the final parable of the Rich Man and Lazarus.

THE PHARISEES REBUKED (LUKE 16:14–18)

In the final section of Luke 14–16 the attention shifts once more to Jesus' opposition. The reference to the ridicule of the Pharisees intimates that

176. Ibid., 52.

they had kept an eye on Jesus and had been listening to his teachings on the wise use of money. Shown in their most direct hostility to Jesus (ἐκμυκτηρίζω, Luke 16:14, expresses strong contempt), they perceived no conflict of interest between piety and the love of money, or, as Luke 16:13 expresses it, God and Mammon.[177] Geldenhuys goes even one step further by saying that they "regarded riches as the rightful reward for faithful observance of the Law,"[178] thereby anticipating the direction in which Jesus' response will proceed. In any case, Marshall notes that the Pharisees and scribes had a reputation for φιλάργυρος[179] ("love of money"). The overall focus on the economic reversal motif from the Magnificat (Luke 1:53) thus continues.

Luke 16:14–31 takes the discussion in a new direction by linking comportment with regard to wealth and concerns with the relevance of the Law. The question of Law obedience connects with the introduction to Luke 14–16 (Luke 14:1–6) and thus brings closure to the three chapters, as the use of possessions and the ethical standards of the Law also form key themes of the concluding parable of the Rich Man and Lazarus. Aside from Torah conformity as the means of establishing personal righteousness (cf. Luke 16:15–16), the references to the Law should not come as a surprise. Concern for the poor and generosity had always been a staple of Torah instruction (cf. Exod 22:25; Exod 23:6, 11; Lev 19:10; Lev 23:22; Lev 25:35; Deut 15:4, 7).

Luke 16:16 has been called "an exegetical minefield"[180] on account of its eschatological division of time into two distinct periods and on account of the meaning of the term βιάζεται. Before these issues can be discussed, a brief survey of Luke 16:14–17 (barring the notoriously difficult Luke 16:18 for the present) is in order. The logic of Jesus' words aims at exposing the Pharisees' breaking of the Law, the very standards they thought they upheld. Their apparent avarice was itself a flagrant transgression of Mosaic stipulations. Luke 16:15 speaks of the self-evaluation of the Pharisees. In the growing conflict of Luke 14–16, they had been judging Jesus as a lawbreaker (Luke 14:1–6), not to speak of their attitude

---

177. Ellis, *The Gospel of Luke*, 202. Jesus' words in Luke 16:10–13 effectively issued a charge of idolatry against anyone who treasures possessions. The Pharisees had no scruples about their relation to wealth, but it would not have occurred to them that they could be idolaters. It is this thought that they object to with such force.

178. Geldenhuys, *Commentary on the Gospel of Luke*, 420.

179. Cf. Marshall, *The Gospel of Luke*, 625.

180. Cf. Bock, *Luke 9:51—24:53*, 1350.

towards the "tax collectors and sinners" (Luke 15:1–2). Yet, they consider themselves as "just" (οἱ δικαιοῦντες ἑαυτοὺς, Luke 16:15), a sentiment evidently shared by the religious community but not by God. The opposite evaluation by God is expressed in the maxim of Luke 16:15b, which forms an echo of Luke 14:11: "What is exalted among men is an abomination in the sight of God." The language also connects with a number of wisdom sayings from Proverbs, especially 16:5: "Everyone who is proud of heart is an abomination to the Lord; be assured he will not go unpunished." What is at stake in this pericope is justice based on the standards of the Law. By these standards, the Pharisees cannot possibly be called just, not only because they exalt themselves, but also because of what their hearts reveal about the love of money. As lovers of money, they are implicated as worshipers of Mammon, which spells idolatry and therefore the transgression of the most fundamental principle of the Law (cf. Deut 5:7). In this regard, it is quite possible that the word "abomination" (βδέλυγμα, Luke 16:15) is invested with the notion of idol worship documented by a number of texts in the LXX (cf. Deut 7:25; Deut 12:31; 1 Kgs 11:6–8; Dan 9:27; Dan 11:31).[181] It is the inherent *in*justice of the proud that Jesus is exposing in this brief interchange with a sense of delicious irony.

Luke 16:16–17 makes explicit that the rule of Law has not and will not be abrogated as the standard of judging a person's behavior, despite the fact that the good news of the kingdom is already published and a new era has superseded the times of the "Law and the Prophets." In light of what Jesus has said about the Pharisees' hearts in Luke 16:15, the general thrust of his words then is to declare the opposition as guilty of breaking the Law, and their verdict will not be reversed until they repent and respond to his preaching of the kingdom of God. With this sharp response, Jesus has moved from the implicit invitation to the Pharisees in the open-ended story of the older son to an unmistakable warning of judgment, which will become even more overt in Luke 16:19–31.

As for the enigmatic saying of Luke 16:16b and its use of βιάζεται, it is this study's contention that the words are best read in conjunction with the previous installments of the ongoing tug-of-war. When viewed against the backdrop of the history of the conflict between Jesus and the Pharisees in chapters 14–16, Luke 16:16–17 gathers up the strains and brings the debate to a preliminary conclusion.[182] The validity and inter-

---

181. Cf. Greene, *The Gospel of Luke*, 602, fn. 314.

182. As will be argued below, the same is true for the saying about divorce and remarriage in Luke 16:18.

pretation of the Law had been the subject of discussion as early as Luke 14:1–6, but Jesus' perceived lack of conformity to Torah standards also consisted in the charge of "receiving sinners and eating with them" (Luke 15:2), namely, a certain inclusiveness which the Pharisees condemned.[183] This aspect of the conflict gives us a clue as to the much-debated force of βιάζεται.

While Matthew's parallel (Luke 11:12) requires a decidedly negative sense for the verb, Luke's version of the saying has elicited a dispute about whether its meaning is to be understood as hostile or positive.[184] "All act violently against it" (i.e., the kingdom, assuming a middle aspect for βιάζεται)[185] seems too negative for the context, since it is only the Pharisees who openly oppose Jesus.[186] On the other hand, Fitzmyer's rendering with the sense of "all are urged to enter,"[187] while making better sense of the utterance's literary setting, is unlikely inasmuch as βιάζεσθαι followed by the preposition εἰς invariably communicates a negative sense, often implying hostile intent ("forcefully to press into," "to fight against").[188]

A negative meaning is best retained, and the construct can be translated, "everyone presses into it." The use of πᾶς comes with the idea of indiscriminateness ("every *kind* of person") and connects with Jesus' habit of welcoming outcasts. From the vantage point of an outside observer, the free offer of the kingdom (albeit always coupled with a call to repentance) appears to democratize access to the God of Israel, as opposed to the cultic strictures of Torah-based Second Temple Judaism with its focus on the many formalized aspects of religion. It is unnecessary to decide whether βιάζεται entails an entry pursued on terms other than God's,[189]

---

183. With respect to Luke 16:16, Greene (*The Gospel of Luke*, 603) takes a similar position. His interpretation of βιάζεται ("everyone is urged to enter"), however, seems to be too soft for the lexical meaning of βιάζω ("to apply force").

184. A bibliography regarding the interpretation of βιάζεται is found in Goulder, *Luke—A New Paradigm, Vol. 2*.

185. Ellis (*The Gospel of Luke*, 203) opts for this reading in close alignment with Matt 11:12.

186. One would also expect an adversative particle (δέ) instead of καί as the conjunction of the two halves of the sentence.

187. Cf. Fitzmyer, *The Gospel According to Luke X–XXIV*, 1117–18. Bock (*Luke 9:51—24:53*, 1353) agrees, along with a number of scholars who affirm a positive sense with varying nuances. For a full-orbed discussion on this reading and additional bibliography see Cortés and Gatti, "On the Meaning of Luke 16:16," 247–59.

188. Cf. the discussion of Schrenk in *THDNT* Vol. 1, 612.

189. Cf. Arndt, *The Gospel According to St. Luke*, 360–62.

Exposition

or simply an unabashed taking advantage of the preaching of the good news and the offer of forgiveness on the part of the penitent, which may have seemed like a sell out to Pharisees and Torah-conscious Jews. The fact is, Jesus *did* call sinners to repentance and left his audience in no doubt as to whether or not he would receive the humble (Luke 14:11). His open, indiscriminate invitation, however, could also render the kingdom vulnerable to abuse, and his enemies certainly found fault with such a liberal offer allowing many to sidestep the requirements of the Law (so they thought).

The reference to "every kind of person" pressing into the kingdom of God thus corresponds with the Pharisees' taking offense at Jesus' policy of inclusiveness (Luke 15:1–2) and a ministry that made the kingdom of God accessible for the marginalized and the outcasts, notwithstanding an open invitation to participate for the whole house of Israel.

This reading of Luke 16:16 differs from the meaning of Matt 11:12, but when we realize that Jesus' use of βιάζεται is intended to mirror the opposition's take on (and possibly language describing) his ministry, the negative force of the construct βιάζεσθαι + εἰς can be retained without having to explain why the phrase shows no adversative particle. We may think of it as an ironic concession on the part of Jesus: "And yes, the people *are* pressing into the kingdom—and you would be better off if you did, too, because you also need God's forgiveness on account of him knowing your hearts. . ."

What then is the logic of Jesus' words up to this point? While the Law used to be the governing standard of Judaism, a new era has dawned that may seem like religion is now available at a discounted price, but in reality (and this explains the presence of Luke 16:17), the moral requirements of the Law will always be the measure by which a life is judged. By the standard of the Law, therefore, the Pharisees, as lovers of money, stand condemned, and everything depends on whether they will humble themselves before God by accepting the message of Jesus. The stage is set for the concluding tale (Luke 16:19–31) of Luke 14–16.

The function and meaning of Luke 16:18 in context remains to be discussed, a question that has produced a multiplicity of suggestions.[190] The contributions can be summarized in terms of four distinct interpretive approaches. Perhaps the most popular exegesis of the divorce saying claims that Luke included it at this point in order to confirm the continu-

---

190. Cf. Kilgallen, "The Purpose of Luke's Divorce Text," 229.

ing validity of the Law, albeit in a new and even more demanding way.[191] After the categorical affirmation of the Law's perpetuity in Luke 16:17, Luke 16:18 would function as a specific illustration of the principle. This view has merit, and it succeeds in explaining why this particular saying was inserted: not only does it affirm the Law, but it even closes the door on the divorce allowance of Deut 24:1–4.[192] There can be no talk of relaxed standards of justice with Jesus.

Grundmann's approach proposes a different logic for the inclusion of the saying.[193] He draws attention to the great importance of monetary issues in the Pharisees successive divorce and re-marriage policies. This interpretation thus links the earlier charge of avarice with the Pharisees' divorce tactics. Grundmann adds a valuable nuance to our understanding of Luke 16:18 in context, but the combination of the two elements is at best only implied, and it does not add much to the force of the argument against the Pharisees.

Another reading has been advanced by L. T. Johnson.[194] He takes his cue from the OT's linking of three cardinal sins (idolatry, greed, sexual immorality/divorce) by the term βδέλυγμα (Luke 16:15). The presence of "abomination" in Luke 16:15 provides the rationale for joining Luke 16:18 to the preceding verses. In other words, with the addition of the divorce saying Jesus issues a full-orbed prophetic charge against the opposition modeled after the language of OT indictments.[195] Βδέλυγμα can function as a code word for idolatry in the LXX (cf. Deut 7:25–26; Deut 12:31; Jer 16:18; Ezek 5:9–11; Dan 9:27). It is also true that this term can signify adultery or fornication, especially *spiritual* adultery, in which case the connection with idolatry is very pronounced (cf. Deut 23:18; Jer 13:27).[196] Moreover, the Pharisees have already been charged with idolatry (at least indirectly) on account of their love of Mammon. Idolatry, in turn, translates into spiritual adultery. Based on these con-

---

191. Cf. Marshall, *The Gospel of Luke*, 631; Klostermann, *Das Lukasevangelium*, 167; Nolland, *Luke 9:21–18:34*, 822.

192. The divorce allowance of Deut 24:1–4 is explicitly mentioned in Mark 10:1–12 and Matt 19:1–9. Both passages contain Jesus' divorce saying with minor variations.

193. Grundmann, *Das Evangelium nach Lukas*, 324.

194. Ibid., 324.

195. Johnson also cites CD 4:14—5:10 as evidence from Qumran that the combination of idolatry, greed, and sexual immorality had found its way into secondary documents (Ibid., 256).

196. This point is also argued by Just, *Luke 9:51—24:53*, 628–29.

siderations, Johnson's approach accounts well for the logic of the inclusion of the divorce saying.

A fourth interpretation sees Luke 16:18 as a figurative statement.[197] Similar to Paul's marriage/divorce metaphor in Rom 7:1–4, Weiss contends that it would be adulterous to wish to continue in a "relationship" with Law after God has already ushered in a new order in Jesus' preaching of the kingdom. It would be tantamount to marrying a divorced wife.[198] This reading lacks sufficient literary justification, a deficit that Kilgallen has tried to remedy in his own figurative reading of Luke 16:18.[199] For him, marriage and divorce are "no longer literal," but figures of speech meant "to show the value of anything that is not to be changed,"[200] in this case, the Law and the Prophets as the effectual "guide to repentance."[201] By emphasizing the continuing role of the Law and the Prophets, Kilgallen's reading harmonizes with the following parable, in which the hearing (and doing) of "Moses and the Prophets" (Luke 16:29, 31) appears to avoid the torments of Hades.

Virtually, all of the above interpretations can make valuable contributions to our understanding of Luke 16:18, and at least views one and four are not mutually exclusive. Nonetheless, the divorce saying, a seemingly stray proverb unexpectedly introduced and abandoned immediately, has yet to be seen in the overall context of the history of the growing conflict of Luke 14–16. It is in this setting that the saying can unfold its fullest rhetorical potential. If Luke is responsible for inserting the saying at this junction in Luke 14–16 (and I would argue he is), then this was done not only to make it interact with the transitional passage of Luke 16:14–18, but to reflect the author's understanding of how the apparently well-known divorce saying could advance the larger conflict of Luke 14–16. In short, Luke 16:18 performs the same function of turning the tables on the accusers which we already observed in Luke 16:15–17.[202] The effect is achieved by the proverb's echoing a salient motif introduced earlier in the debate between Jesus and the Pharisees.

---

197. Cf. Weiss, *Markus und Lukas*, 547–48; Jülicher, *Die Gleichnisreden Jesu*, 633.

198. Weiss, *Markus und Lukas*, 548.

199. Kilgallen, "The Purpose of Luke's Divorce Text," 231–38.

200. Ibid., 236.

201. Ibid., 238.

202. *Pace*, Kilgallen, who argues that Luke 16:18 "certainly is not accusing the Pharisees of guilt in this matter" ("The Purpose," 237).

In his denunciation of his younger brother (Luke 15:29–30), the recalcitrant elder son speaks with the voice of the Pharisees in the parable of the Prodigal. In particular his (unfounded) charge of association with prostitutes served to recall the Pharisees' objection that Jesus received "sinful people" (Luke 15:2; cf. also Luke 7:36–50). Seen as a statement of anaphoric import, Luke 16:18 mirrors their objection against the immoral and returns the verdict upon their own heads. If at least the school of Hillel advocated divorce and remarriage for reasons other than specified in Deut 24:1–4, then those who taught and practiced this tradition are hereby pronounced adulterers.

A quick reference to Luke 18:9–14 reveals that in the parable of the Pharisee and the Tax Collector the contrast between the self-righteous (Pharisee) and the sinful is built upon the same twofold accusation brought against the Pharisees in Luke 16:14–18, namely, greed and adultery.[203] It is clear, too, that with this indirect accusation looming over the Pharisees, they could be classified as "outcasts" on much the same grounds that they rejected the lawless libertines. They must not only repent of their avarice, but also of their sexual immorality. The irony of their situation is that their interpretation of the Law both oppressed the needy (cf. Luke 14:1–6, i.e., Law and its exegetical tradition became a tool for oppression) as well as placed the leaders themselves under the verdict of the Law as idolaters and adulterers.[204] Humiliation (cf. Luke 14:11; Luke 16:19–31) is inevitable, barring the possibility of repentance.

Before we leave this passage, I may point out that Luke 16:18 with its implicit charge of adultery also connects with the wisdom theme of the foolish son we discussed with respect to Luke 15:29–30. More generally, the fool of wisdom literature predictably winds up in an adulterous affair (Prov 2:16–19; Prov 5:1–6; Prov 6:24–35; Prov 7:5–27; Prov 9:13–18; Prov 23:26–28), and so "in the depths of Sheol" (Prov 9:18), a movement ominous of the rich man in Luke 16:19–31. The reference is designated to turn the tables on the accusers.

---

203. Avarice is present in the word "extortioners" (possibly also in "tax collector"), while another cause for "thankfulness" on the part of the Pharisee is that he is not an "adulterer" (Luke 18:11).

204. Cf. Bindemann, "Ungerechte als Vorbilder?" 967.

7. THE RICH MAN AND LAZARUS (LUKE 16:14-18)

The closing parable of Luke 14–16 performs a double function as both the climax of Jesus' speech against the love of money[205] and the final word in his ongoing controversy with the Pharisees (and scribes).[206] The conduct of the rich man stands in stark opposition to the shrewdness of the unjust steward, whom Luke 16:9 holds up as an example to follow. A comparison of the two stories already seems promising in that the opening formula ἄνθρωπος δέ τις ἦν πλούσιος is identical to Luke 16:1. The rich man, in later literature often referred to as *Dives* (from Latin, "rich"),[207] serves as a perfect type of wealth, signified both by his wardrobe as well as his luxurious feasting.[208] However, whereas the unjust steward employed money wisely, the rich man is deserving of the epithet "fool" (cf. Luke 12:13–21). His careless attitude spells misuse of wealth, and he miserably fails in gaining access to "eternal dwellings" (Luke 16:9).[209]

As Snodgrass rightly observes,[210] the gate at which Lazarus was laid is symbolical of the separation that exists between the rich, who feasted sumptuously on one side of it, and Lazarus, who perished on the other. While the gate should have been an aperture through which mercy (cf. Luke 16:24) could be extended to the poor wretch (the rich man was surely not ignorant of Lazarus), it becomes an ominous sign of the permanent chasm fixed between the two after death. The reversal of Luke 1:52–53 is beckoning (cf. also Luke 6:20–21) with the impossibility of passage (cf. Luke 16:26) from one sphere to another: the poor remains blessed, and the rich remains "empty" because he refused to make "friends

---

205. Hendrickx, *The Parables of Jesus*, 199.

206. Cf. Eckey, *Das Lukasevangelium*, II, 717.

207. Marshall (*The Gospel of Luke*, 634) offers a summary view of the various titles used of the rich man in secondary literature.

208. Cf. Forbes, *God of Old*, 185.

209. The question as to whether the detailed account of the deceased characters is merely ornamental or whether it should be taken more seriously as a depiction of the afterlife has been debated at length. The issue is peripheral for the present study. A full-fledged summary of the history of interpretation is found in Lehtipuu's dissertation. She posits a *via media* view on the issue. The story's rendering of the afterlife is not an essential component of Luke's eschatology, yet it cannot be simply dismissed as a piece of imagination. The story has a decidedly dark edge, which is lost when its depiction of the hereafter becomes no more than a creative *tour de force*. Cf. Lehtipuu, *The Afterlife Imagery*.

210. Snodgrass, *Stories with Intent*, 423–24.

with unrighteous Mammon" (Luke 16:9) in low places. This failure also indicates that he did not listen to Moses (cf. Luke 16:29–31).

Thus both parables in Luke 16, one positively, one negatively, draw from the saying of Luke 16:9 as a common center of gravity.[211] But the importance of "friends" in the kingdom of God is also consistent with the teachings of Luke 14:12–14, where the invitation of "the poor, the crippled, the lame, and the blind" promises a divine welcome "at the resurrection of the just."[212] The parable of the Rich Man and Lazarus in particular addresses another point of contention already raised in connection with the Great Banquet, namely, the error of a false sense of election, according to which no "son of Abraham" could possibly end up among the rejected and so fail to "eat bread in the kingdom of God" (Luke 14:15). The rich man's repeated address of Abraham from Hades as his "father" (Luke 16:24, 30) injects a conspicuous element of drama into the story and would have raised eyebrows among the original Jewish listeners who had "Abraham as father" (cf. Luke 3:8–9). The warning of Luke 14:15–24 is thus reinforced.

Beyond this, we may not overlook details in the Rich Man and Lazarus which resonate with both Luke 14:1–6 and Luke 14:7–11, reaching all the way to the beginning of the larger text block of Luke 14–16 and adding to the sense of closure this parable affords. As has been noted by several commentators,[213] the peculiar phrase "Abraham's bosom" (Luke 16:22, unknown elsewhere in Jewish literature) suggests a banquet scene with Lazarus as the guest of honor reclining next to the host Abraham. In this sense, Lazarus' movement from the gutter to his final destination at the heavenly banquet echoes the ascent of the lowly described in the wisdom instruction of Luke 14:7–11.

The rich man's request for a sensational miraculous sign also affords an ironic link with the miracle story, which served as the opening text for Luke 14–16. While he protests that Moses and the Prophets are not enough for his brothers to put them on the path of repentance, Luke

---

211. This insight I have gathered from Ball, "The Parables of the Unjust Steward," 329–30.

212. The story's detail of Lazarus being "laid" at the gate (Luke 16:20, ἐβέβλητο) underscores his helplessness and intimates that he also qualified as "lame" (possibly "crippled," cf. Luke 14:13) or at least immobile. Lazarus appears to embody most of the catalogue of ailments described in Luke 14:13.

213. Cf. Tannehill, *Luke*, 252; Forbes, *God of Old*, 188–89; Hendrickx, *The Parables of Jesus*, 202; Stein, *Luke*, 424.

Exposition

14:1–6 already established the sad fact that the "lawyers and Pharisees" did not only not listen to the Law (and the Prophets) but could not be reached by a miraculous intervention either. They hardened their hearts against the truth of God in both Word and sign. The parable of the Rich Man and Lazarus completes the downward movement for the proud in suggesting that they will experience the ultimate humiliation in Hades—unless they repent.

The Rich Man and Lazarus evinces notable links with the Lost Sons, too (Luke 15:11–32). Both stories are double-edged, in that they feature two segments, with the emphasis being on the second part.[214] The two-part structure can be represented in the following way:

1. Repentance & Reversal (Luke 15:11–24)	1. The Great Reversal (Luke 16:19–26)
2. Elder Brother Hardened (Luke 15:25–32)	2. Refusal to Hear Moses (Luke 16:27–31)

Both parables' endings also sustain a certain lingering bite by drawing the reader into the story. The Lost Sons closes with a recalcitrant brother who is entreated by his loving father. Will he join the festivities after all? The rich man's brothers have the passionate entreaties and warnings of Moses and the Prophets, but will they take notice? The conclusion of the dialogue between the rich man and Abraham renders a skeptical view of the possibility of repentance on the part of the unsuspecting brothers (Luke 16:29–31). Nonetheless, the matter remains open, and in this sense the challenge is laid before the reader who has the Law and the Prophets. More so, an allusion to Christ as one greater than Lazarus having come back from the dead could not be missed by Luke's readers.[215]

Further points of contact between the two parables deserve mentioning.[216] Distance is a metaphor for being lost in both stories. The rich man "saw Abraham far off" (Luke 16:23, ἀπὸ μακρόθεν), and the prodigal son was sighted by his father "yet being far away" (Luke 15:20, μακρὰν ἀπέχοντος, cf. also Luke 15:13). Of course, the χάσμα separating the rich

---

214. As Talbert has noted (*Reading Luke*, 188), in double-edged parables it is the second part that ordinarily carries the story's *Pointe* (cf. also Petzke, *Das Sondergut*, 149).

215. So Forbes, *God of Old*, 194.

216. Hintzen, *Verkündigung und Wahrnehmung*, 360, anticipates much of what is said here in his examination of shared motifs in the stories of the Rich Man and Lazarus and the Lost Sons. For Hintzen, the parallel features of the parables betray their common source or tradition.

man and Lazarus is fixed and cannot be bridged, while the younger son is about to be received by his loving father, thereby eliminating the distance and isolation brought about by sin.

Hunger and deprivation also link the stories in that both Lazarus and the prodigal "desire to be filled" (Luke 15:16, ἐπεθύμει χορτασθῆναι; Luke 16:21, ἐπιθυμῶν χορτασθῆναι). Both face the indignity of being in contact with unclean animals (Luke 15:15; Luke 16:21), which in either case reinforces the derelict position held by the miserable.

The emphatic address of the father to his recalcitrant son (Luke 15:31, τέκνον) is matched verbatim by Abraham's response to the rich man's appeal from Hades (Luke 16:25), and both vocatives are followed by reminders about "your things."[217] The language of fatherhood connects with the Lost Sons in a more general sense. Three times Abraham is invoked with pathos (πάτερ, Luke 16:24, 27, 30), but despite acknowledging the rich man as his child (Luke 16:25), Abraham cannot grant any of the rich man's requests.[218] Kinship is thus acknowledged, but it will not afford deliverance without a life of compassion. Abraham's retort reminding the rich man of "your good things" received in life suggests that the rich man had obtained what he had *chosen* for himself: a luxurious life centered on self-gratification with little or no concern for the less privileged.

Bauckham challenges the consensus that the reversal for the rich man is based on his lack of concern for the poor or the injustice of unequal distribution of wealth.[219] The proximity of Lazarus to the rich man (at his very gate) already strongly suggests that the rich man *should* have done something to alleviate his suffering. And if the rich man's conduct is not responsible for his rejection, his own words of repentance (Luke 16:27–30) appear to be strangely disconnected from the first part of the parable. Although the rich man's misconduct is only implicit, the reader is to come to this conclusion in consideration of the story as a whole.

Repentance constitutes another motif common to both parables. In the parable of the Rich Man and Lazarus, the lack of repentance provides the rationale for the reversal experienced by the rich man. He wants Lazarus to be sent to his five unsuspecting (and apparently unrepentant) brothers, for if they should listen to his warnings, "they

---

217. Both arguments are aiming at making the other see that what is happening is right. For the elder brother see Hendrickx, *The Parables of Jesus*, 205.

218. Cf. Tannehill, *Luke*, 253.

219. Bauckham, "The Rich Man and Lazarus," 236.

will repent" (Luke 16:29). The younger son's reversal of fortune rests precisely on his return to his father's homestead, which is to be read through the lens of the shorter parables in chapter 15 (Luke 15:1–10) as a salient picture of repentance.

The fact that the rich man desires to have one from the dead go to his brothers (Luke 16:30) also relates to the Lost Sons. Here, the return of the younger son is captured in a metaphor of his having been dead and yet having come to life again (Luke 15:31). The portrait of the son returning from death is intended to give the elder a "living" cause to repent of his hardness of heart. Even though the father speaks only analogically, in the parable of the Rich Man and Lazarus the request of sending a "real" man from the dead is put before Abraham, and it is denied. Through these Abraham's words, then, Jesus addresses himself to the Pharisees, who have Moses and the Prophets. If they would only listen to them, never mind a message from a resuscitated man, they would have repented. They have not listened, and therefore continue in their present conduct.

The theme of celebration affords yet another common feature. A celebration is announced at the return of the son (Luke 15:23, 24, 32, εὐφραίνω), while the rich man celebrates (Luke 16:19, εὐφραίνω) luxuriously from day to day. Both parables also note the issue of extravagant clothing in the very context of celebration (Luke 15:22; Luke 16:19). In the case of the prodigal, the rejoicing is part and parcel of the path of repentance. In the parable of the Rich Man and Lazarus the rejoicing is frontloaded in order to turn into mourning for lack of concern for the poor.

The complex literary and thematic relationships between the main stories of Luke 14–16 aim at assisting the reading in seeing the concept of reversal of fortunes from a variety of different angles. Nevertheless, all of the material goes back to the twofold reversal stated in Luke 1:51–53, which is also reflected in the beatitudes of Luke 6:20–21, 24–25. The group experiencing a negative reversal includes the proud (Luke 1:51, or those who "laugh," Luke 6:25b) and the rich (Luke 1:52–53; Luke 6:24–25a), whereas the poor (Luke 1:52–53; Luke 6:20b–21) and the humble mourners (Luke 1:52b; Luke 6:21b) will be exalted. Jesus' opponents identify with the former class, whereas the disciples identify with the latter, or are called upon to do so. While the reversal motif is pronounced in the Rich Man and Lazarus, the presence of wisdom concepts remains to be probed.

At the Heart of Luke

The care and concern for the poor is a staple of wisdom literature, and not only of Jewish origin.[220] An ample amount of wisdom instruction commends generosity toward the poor as counting for righteousness and the fear of the Lord. Prov 14:31 may be cited as representative of the wealth of sayings preoccupied with the same subject: "Whoever oppresses a poor man insults his Maker, but he who is generous to the needy honors him." Likewise, Prov 19:17: "whoever is generous to the poor lends to Yahweh, and he will repay him for his deed." The link between deeds of mercy for the poor and divine retribution is as pronounced as in Jesus' sayings from Luke 14:13–14 as well as the parable of the Rich Man and Lazarus, which may be regarded as a vivid illustration of the promise of a reward in the resurrection (Luke 14:14), though the parable falls short of speaking of resurrection proper. Additional proverbial wisdom hits this note in recommending care for the underprivileged (Prov 11:24–26; Prov 17:5; Prov 21:26; Prov 22:9; Prov 28:27; Prov 29:7, etc.).

In Job's summary defense before his three friends (Job 29:11–16) the main point affirming his righteousness rests on Job's sharing his bread with the poor and extending mercy to the outcasts. Even the less conventional wisdom of Qoheleth calls for generosity (Eccl 11:1–2).

Two extra-canonical wisdom works promote the care for the poor in no uncertain terms. In particular Wisd. 2:1—3:12 speaks the reversal language of the parable of the Rich Man and Lazarus. The ungodly (Luke 2:1) "oppress the poor righteous man" (Luke 2:10–11) but come to a violent end (Luke 3:10–12), whereas the poor righteous, after having been chastised (Luke 3:5) will eventually be visited by God and "shine" in glory (Luke 3:7). Similarly, Ben Sirach exalts the virtue of mercy and generosity, especially for the poor (Luke 29:1–2, 10, 22), howbeit without being explicit in promising a reward in the afterlife. Law and Wisdom thus coincide in enjoining the relief of the poor as a core characteristic of the righteous/wise (cf. Deut 15:4). Yahweh is opposed to the exalted and self-sufficient who are insensitive to the poor.

Conversely, if wealth offers no guarantee of God's approval in the absence of a merciful attitude, then poverty is no proof of one's rejection. While wisdom literature does teach that prosperity is a sign of blessing (Prov 10:22), it also speaks of the piety of the poor who trust in Yahweh: "Better is a little with the fear of Yahweh than great treasure and trouble with it" (Prov 15:16; cf. Prov 15:17; Prov 16:8; Prov 17:1, etc.).

---

220. Talbert, *Reading Luke*, 186.

Exposition

God's identification with the poor in the parable appears to be intimated in the naming of the beggar as Lazarus. Assuming that the hearers understood its meaning ("God helps"), the name is given so as not to "permit the hearer to think Lazarus is cursed because of his condition."[221] He may be miserable but the happy end of his life story shows that God had always been on his side.[222] As Forbes rightly notes,[223] the poor man's name betokens the reversal of fortune which unfolds in the parable. Not to over-interpret the name, it may be pointed out that the LXX translates its Hebrew root עזר ("to help," as in אלעזר, Lazarus) with ἀντιλαμβάνω in passages that mention God as the "helper" of the needy (Ps 118:13; 1 Chr 22:17). The verb is also found in the Magnificat (Luke 1:54), triumphing in the Lord who "has *helped* his servant Israel, in remembrance of his mercy." Even though no one else helped Israel, the Lord has, and his mercy designates his ability to associate with the lowly (cf. Luke 1:48). Lazarus' position of honor in Abraham's bosom at the heavenly banquet would be illustrative of this notion, and it is possible that Luke included the name not only to prepare the reader for the reversal in the parable, but also in view of the reversal theme in the Magnificat, concluding with the servant Israel having been "helped" (i.e., saved) by the Lord.

The parable's chronicle of the rich man bears resemblance with the rich "fool" of Luke 12:13–21, another wisdom parable. The difference lies in the latter tale's focus on the ostentatious pride and hoarding of the fool (enough is never enough), while the rich man of Luke 16:19–31 is characterized by careless self-gratification. But as one who refused to listen to Moses and the Prophets, not to speak of the voice of wisdom summarized above, he too has earned the dubious epithet of the "fool." His wisdom would have been to make friends with his wealth. The parable's proximity to the Unjust Steward as a wisdom parable already suggests its classification as a wisdom story. The rich man is thus an antihero exhibiting the characteristics of the "fool."

---

221. Snodgrass, *Stories with Intent*, 429.
222. Cf. also Forbes, *God of Old*, 186.
223. Ibid., 186.

4

Wisdom as Calculation and Humility in Light of God's Activity

ISRAEL'S SAGES PROPAGATE THE fear of Yahweh as the beginning or first principle of wisdom. All aspects of life and creation are traced to God's creative fiat (Prov 3:19) and invite study in a spirit of humility so as to take one's due place within the world.[1] While the rudimentary principles of wisdom remain intact, the advent of Jesus and the preaching of the kingdom also change man's situation in the world. Jesus' teaching comes with the demand for a decision. The Magnificat portrays God's salvation as an eschatological reversal. Thus the sovereign act of God forms the apex of Luke's theology. Those who hear the "good news of the kingdom of God" preached (Luke 16:16) experience the reversal in one of two ways. They either participate in the reversal by humbling themselves, or they refuse in order to *be* humbled in the end. The parables of Luke 14–16 and the illustrative conflict informing the text block suggest that the pride of the latter party is to construed specifically in terms of having heard the voice of God but not heeding it (Luke 14:15–23; Luke 15:25–32; Luke 16:27–31). In this sense, those who "exalt" themselves also become (involuntary) participants in the reversal that God brings about through his servant Jesus. The good news of the kingdom can result in a hardening of hearts resulting in judgment. The wisdom maxim of Luke 14:11 is

---

1. Cf. Kidner, *The Wisdom of Proverbs*, 12.

Wisdom as Calculation and Humility in Light of God's Activity

the epitome of this principle. In light of the coming of the kingdom in Jesus, those who humble themselves will be exalted, and those who exalt themselves (against this Word of the kingdom) will be humbled.

So the wisdom motifs deposited in the parables and teachings of Luke 14–16 recommend active participation through humbling oneself and warn against failure to do so. Two basic ideas define the wisdom quest for the reader. Prerequisite for receiving the wisdom that both the stories and teachings seek to impart is the realization of the worthiness of Jesus (Luke 14:26–27) and the promise of the eschatological banquet (Luke 14:7–24). It is thus not at all accidental that we find these concepts featured near the beginning of the text block. The question of priorities is the gateway into Luke 14–16.[2] The invitation to the banquet will not be turned down if its importance is seen as an ultimatum (cf. Luke 14:18–20). The call to discipleship also involves a counting of costs: One must be ready for a radical commitment to Jesus (Luke 14:25–35). Behind all this looms the notion of the worthiness of God as the host of the banquet and the sender of Jesus. Although the idea surfaces only at one point (Luke 16:13, loving God and not mammon as Master), aspects of the person and character of God are revealed in virtually all of the parables as the unifying theme of not only chapters 14–16, but all of the Lukan *Sondergut* parables.[3] The worthiness of the goal entails its weighing against anything that might stand in the way of pursuing the promise on the part of the reader. The most overt reference to such calculation is, of course, found in the short wisdom parables of the Tower Builder and the King Going to War (Luke 14:28–32) followed by the interpretive saying of Luke 14:33.[4] It is only after recognizing the kingdom and the person of Jesus as the most desirable good, that one can commit the resources required to pursuing the goal.

---

2. In the parables of the Lost (in particular Luke 15:1–10) the focus shifts from the disciple's recognition of the worthiness of both Jesus and the kingdom to God's joy over "one sinner who repents" (15:7, 10). God's joy over the penitent is said to exceed the joy he entertains over the "ninety-nine righteous persons" (15:7). Heavenly joy is a barometer for the significance and value of the penitent in the eyes of God. This notion is the flipside of the disciple's affirmation of Jesus and the kingdom taking priority in everything.

3. Forbes argues this point convincingly (*God of Old*, 248–57).

4. Cf. Prov 20:18: "Plans are established by counsel; by wise guidance wage war." This proverb could well have been the conceptual starting point of Jesus' twin stories of Luke 14:28–32.

If participation in the kingdom and discipleship of Jesus are the end of the wisdom taught in Luke 14–16, then the best (or rather, only) means of realization is to "take the lowest place" (Luke 14:10).[5] Wisdom, humility, and repentance thus form a string of very closely related or nearly synonymous thoughts. Humility is the virtue that already takes center stage in Jesus' table-talk (Luke 14:7ff.), culminating in the momentous saying of Luke 14:11. The sapiential instruction of Luke 14:7–11 banks on humility as the single most desirable character trait of those who heed Jesus' wisdom.

But humility as the hallmark of the wisdom of Jesus' teaching certainly translates into repentance. The words of Luke 14:12–14 intimate a change of heart for most (if not all hearers) who are entrenched in a system of reciprocity. Here it is not the "worthies" of society who ought to be honored with an invitation, but the "un-worthies" described in the catalogue of Luke 14:13. Repentance and humility may thus be linked insofar as the former demands a willingness to humble oneself by associating with the down and out who will not be able to benefit the generous in this life. Yet, this is a small price to pay in light of the promised "repayment" (cf. Luke 14:14) at the resurrection of the just. So long as the promised reward is deemed worthy enough, repentance and humility will follow suit.

The concept of repentance as an aspect of wisdom is then further developed in Luke 15:11–32.[6] As we have shown in the previous chapter, the prodigal's coming to himself (Luke 15:17) is the beginning of a journey back home, which is as much an act of genuine repentance as it is one of new-found humility.[7] The prodigal's wisdom is seen in his repentance: "Whoever gets sense loves his own soul" (Prov 19:8). And "the reward for humility and the fear of Yahweh is riches and honor and life" (Prov 22:4). Significantly, the father's comment on his son's repentance employs the metaphor of returning to life (Luke 15:24, 32). In wisdom literature,

---

5. This concept of wisdom defined as goal in relation to means of realization corresponds with Charnock's masterful analysis of wisdom in *The Existence and Attributes of God*, 507.

6. Wisdom as entailing the departure from sin is a well-documented sapiential theme, as will be shown below (cf. Job 28:28; Prov 3:7; Prov 8:13; Prov 16:6; Eccl 7:4–5; Eccl 8:11–13).

7. As argued in chapter 3 of this work, the son's proposition to be received as a hireling (Luke 15:19) gives expression to how the son is taking the lowest position based on his perceived intrinsic unworthiness (cf. "I am no longer *worthy* . . .," Luke 15:19), whereupon the father exalts him, thus completing the reversal of Luke 14:11b.

Wisdom as Calculation and Humility in Light of God's Activity

the path of wisdom is one that "leads to life" (Prov 3:18; Prov 13:14; Prov 14:27; Prov 19:23).[8]

In Luke 16, the calculation of cost in relation to the desired goal resurfaces with a special focus on the use of money, corresponding to the second reversal motif from the Magnificat (Luke 1:53). The shrewd manager's wisdom is his foresight and his resolve to commit resources towards "making friends." The point of the parable (Luke 16:1–8) does not rest on whether or not the manager's schemes are ethically commendable, and the master's positive comment (Luke 16:8a) requires no such decision on the part of the reader.[9] As a parable of wisdom, the story introduces the manager's crisis and the means of navigating the danger. In his most difficult situation, he works towards the goal of being received into "houses" (Luke 16:4), and his plan is to ingratiate the debtors for future reciprocation. His wisdom comes with a reward. Jesus' comments (Luke 16:9–13) crystallize the central message of the parable: "make friends for yourselves of unrighteous wealth" (Luke 16:9). "For yourselves" identifies the beneficiary, and the reward of generosity spells reception into "eternal dwellings."

Thus, while Luke 14:12–14 goes against the grain of a system or an agenda of reciprocity, the wisdom of the unjust steward does not constitute an ironic negation of earlier teachings on humility. The crux of the matter lies in the location and the timing of the reward. One is not to pursue a return of favors on earth but aim at reception into a heavenly reality, which in any case implies willingness to put up with a delay until the time of fulfillment.

Even though Jesus' commentary does not identify what might happen if one refuses to take account of the teaching of the parable, the concluding story (Luke 16:19–31) affords a window into the tragic fate of one who acted like a fool in his self-absorbed feasting. Jesus' appeal to show concern for the poor and the consequences that come in the wake of one's response (positive or negative) is a staple of conventional wisdom lore.[10]

---

8. See the discussion on pp 72–73.

9. Although, as argued in the previous chapter of this work, there are good reasons to suggest the manager acted out of bounds of what was considered morally commendable.

10. The parable's explicit concern with "Moses and the Prophets" (Luke 16:29, 31) rather than wisdom does not bar the search for wisdom motifs. Law and wisdom were closely linked in ancient Israel. The fear of Yahweh as the controlling principle of wisdom already assumes the covenantal relationship between God and Israel on account of the use of the covenantal name. The Sinaitic covenant, and indeed all of

One's relation to the underprivileged promises reward for the merciful who associate with the poor and threatens judgment for the unmerciful. The wise is to take account of the consequences and act in accord with the fear of Yahweh. The following references provide some illustration: "My son, defraud not the poor of his living, and make not the needy eyes to wait long. Make not the hungry soul sorrowful" (Ben Sirach 4:1–2; cf. also Ben Sir. 13:19–20; Ben Sir. 16:22–23; Ben Sir. 29:1–3, 10–12). "One gives freely, yet grows all the richer; another withholds what he should give, and only suffers want" (Prov 11:24; cf. also Prov 3:27–28). "Whoever despises his neighbor is a sinner, but blessed is he who is generous to the poor" (Prov 14:21). "Whoever is generous to the poor lends to Yahweh, and he will repay him for his deed" (Prov 19:17). "Whoever gives to the poor will not want, but he who hides his eyes will get many a curse" (Prov 28:27; cf. also Prov 25:21–22; Prov 29:7; Job 29:11–16).

The idea of a process of valuation or calculation is central to the quest of wisdom in more general terms, too. Ben Sirach 6:23–31 advocates the acquisition of wisdom, since it will dress the wise person like a "robe of honor" and deliver a precious "crown of joy" (Ben Sir. 6:31). By the same token, wisdom in Proverbs is to be counted "more precious than jewels" (Prov 3:15). One is to prize wisdom highly (Prov 4:8), and nothing that one may desire in this world can compare to it (Prov 8:11).

However, the close linkage of wisdom, humility, and repentance, so evident in the teachings of Luke 14–16, is also a characteristic of the body of Jewish wisdom literature. The magisterial "fear of Yahweh" as the governing principle of wisdom already spells teachability and therefore entails both humility and repentance (cf. Prov 1:7). Prov 3:7 makes explicit the close connection between wisdom as the fear of Yahweh and repentance: ". . . fear Yahweh, and turn away from evil." Prov 8:13 even speaks of "hatred of evil" as defining the fear of God, language that also appears in Ben Sirach 17:24–26 (cf. also Ben Sir. 35:14). Repentance as a hallmark characteristic of wisdom shows in Prov 16:6: ". . . by the fear of Yahweh one turns away from evil." Most explicit is the link between wisdom and repentance in Job 28:28: "Behold, the fear of the Lord, that is wisdom, and to turn away from evil is understanding."

God's revelation to his people (cf. Prov 9:10; Prov 30:5–6) is thus foundational to the concept of wisdom in the OT. The linking of Law and wisdom is always implicit and at times rather pronounced in wisdom literature (Prov 2:1; Prov 3:1; 6:23; 7:1–2; 13:13; Ben Sirach 9:15; 29:1; 31:13–17; 35:14–15; 36:1–2; 39:1–5).

Wisdom as Calculation and Humility in Light of God's Activity

The nexus of wisdom and humility in sapiential works is even more pronounced. It looms large in the teachings of Ben Sirach. Ben Sirach 3:20 declares that the Lord is "honored by the humble" (cf. also Ben Sir. 32:17), and Ben Sir. 15:8 positions wisdom "far from pride." "Pride was not made for man" (Ben Sir. 10:18) and is hateful before God (Ben Sir. 10:7). Ben Sir. 6:2–3 warns against self-exaltation and its destructive consequences. In biblical wisdom literature, "humility comes before honor" (Prov 15:33; Prov 18:12) as a defining quality of the fear of the Lord. The virtually synonymous humility and fear of Yahweh are juxtaposed in Prov 22:4: "The reward of humility and the fear of Yahweh is riches and honor and life." Humility is integral to the fear of God, as it is to the wisdom concepts in Luke 14–16.

Insofar as the travel narrative and Luke 14–16 in particular serve to lay the theological foundation for the gospel and the passion narrative, the presence of these wisdom themes in Luke 14–16 proffers ground for reflection on the grand finale of the gospel, the crucifixion and resurrection of Christ. After all, the wisdom taught in Jesus' parables is not merely descriptive of the way the disciples must go, but it is enshrined in his life and most of all his death, that is, he *is* the wisdom of God in person.[11]

Wisdom's rudimental underlying principle, the fear of the Lord, places the person of God both at the center and as the ultimate goal of the quest. The fear of God thus bespeaks one's desire to bring glory to God.[12] God's glory is the august purpose of human life, and Jesus, obsessed with the glory of God, pursued this goal relentlessly all the way to his crucifixion. Jesus' wisdom was first expressed in Luke's inclusion of the episode of the boy in the temple (Luke 2:41–51), in which the 12-year-old professed that his life belonged to his Father (Luke 2:49). The account closes with a comment on Jesus' increasing wisdom and favor with God and man (Luke 2:52).

His sole desire to see God glorified reached its most mature expression in his final ordeal. Despite the awful nature of the hour, his basic orientation remained "not my will, but yours, be done" (Luke 22:42). In

---

11. Apparently, this is what Paul believed when he perceived the mystery of God to be "Christ, in whom are hidden all the treasures of wisdom and knowledge" (Col 2:3). In the Corinthian correspondence, he is the "power of God and the wisdom of God" (1 Cor 1:24; cf. 1Cor 1:30; 222:6–7).

12. Piper claims that "divine wisdom begins consciously with God, is consciously sustained by God, and has the glory of God as its conscious goal" (*The Pleasures of God*, 272).

At the Heart of Luke

these words uttered in the garden of Gethsemane the humility of wisdom rises to the surface. If the glory of God defined the end of Jesus' wisdom, the means by which he realized it was the outpouring of himself to God, the act of ultimate self-abasement inherent in the cross. To the degree that he humbled himself, Jesus also exalted God, which is at the heart of the fear of God. In his passion Jesus fulfilled the paradigmatic wisdom principle of Luke 14:11: He humbled himself before God (and man) in order to experience the ignominious death of the cross.

The promised exaltation of the wisdom maxim occurred in the resurrection. Significantly, Luke is the only gospel author who chose to include the rather perplexing exchange unfolding between one of the two criminals crucified alongside the Lord and Jesus himself (Luke 23:39–43). In this brief dialogue, the exaltation of Jesus is anticipated as a "coming into your kingdom"[13] (Luke 23:42). The episode is important for Luke for several reasons.

First of all, the text relates a recognition scene from the most crucial moment of Jesus' ministry.[14] In one last snapshot from the cross Luke delivers the truth hidden from others, yes, even Jesus' own disciples at the time, namely that the shameful death and humiliation of the King of the Jews does not contradict or terminate his claim to royalty. In fact, the criminal's request is for royal clemency "when you come into your kingdom."[15] This intimates that Jesus' humiliation is the means or the way by which the King is to be exalted in order to obtain his kingdom. The wisdom principle of Luke 14:11 beckons.

Jesus' reply to the criminal's pleading is stunning, too. The "when . . ." is rather vague, pointing to some day or time in the future. But the request is granted "today" (σήμερον, Luke 23:43) and even includes Jesus' own person ("you will be *with me* in Paradise"). Jesus himself was to enter Paradise on that very day. The meaning of παράδεισος is, of course, not

---

13. Some manuscripts (א, A, W, *f*1, *f*13, syr), including the Byzantine texts, read, "when you come in your kingdom" (ὅταν ἔλθῃς ἐν τῇ βασιλείᾳ σου), a reference to Christ's return in glory. However, a rich textual fabric of references to the exaltation of Jesus to the right hand of divine royal power already exists in the immediate context of the criminal's request (Luke 19:12; 20:17, 42–43; 22:29–30, 69; 24:26). This emphasis continues into Luke's second volume (Acts 2:29–36). The request is best read in this sense, i.e., in terms of Jesus' resurrection and exaltation/ascension. See Metzger's discussion on this reading in *Commentary*, 181.

14. Cf. Tannehill, *Luke*, 343.

15. Stein, *Luke*, 592–93.

synonymous with "kingdom."[16] Jesus did not enter his kingdom on the day of his death, for his reign did not commence until after his bodily resurrection and ascension to heaven. Nonetheless, he entered into an intermediate state in which he was conscious of God's blessing.[17] As the end of his suffering, his death did not bring any further delay of blessing. Rather, having humbled himself he would also promptly be received into eternal habitations.

The contiguous present of Jesus' "today" is reminiscent of the immediacy of Lazarus' reception to the heavenly banquet upon his death (Luke 16:22). Interestingly, Arndt relates the meaning of Paradise to Abraham's bosom (cf. Luke 16:22-23).[18] In both cases, the sufferer was ushered to a celestial place of bliss without any detainment. Jesus' death as the lowest point in his career was the ultimate expression of his humble wisdom. But he did not have to wait for the reversal that wisdom held out for him. His reception into Paradise was prompt, and his expectation was not to be disappointed.

Jesus' "today" also gave the criminal the promise that he would not have to wait long for the favor he sought from him. Apart from his recognition that the cross was not the end of Jesus' rightful messianic claim, the man himself becomes an example of the qualities that wisdom has been shown to combine. Whatever brought about his change of heart, he no longer haggles about his guilt and its consequences. His free and simple admission of being justly condemned to death evinces the same attitude seen in the prodigal son of Luke 15. He even speaks of his "deserts" by using the same word (ἄξιος, Luke 23:41; cf. Luke 15:19, 21) the prodigal employed characterizing his "worthlessness" in his confession before the father. The son's return to the father's home was an act of genuine repentance which constitutes a distinct property of wisdom. The same is true for the crucified criminal, in whose person the theme of repentance is once more reinforced in dramatic fashion.

The movement toward humbling oneself, however, would be incomplete without the culprit's placing himself unreservedly at the mercy of

---

16. In Judaism, παράδεισος had come to refer to the place or habitation of the righteous dead. It was here that disembodied souls would find their rest in the presence of God prior to the day of the resurrection. Cf. 1 Enoch 17–19; 32:3; 61:12; 2 Enoch 65:10; T. Levi 18:10–11; Ps. Sol. 14:3. The word also appears in two other NT texts (2 Cor 12:4; Rev 2:7), where it has a synonymous meaning.

17. Cf. Bock, *Luke 9:51—24:53*, 1857.

18. Arndt, *The Gospel According to St. Luke*, 471.

Jesus, expressed in his request to be "remembered" (cf. also Luke 1:54b). And just as the father received his son without hesitation, so also Paradise is promised to be his "today." The man's penitent humility stands in sharp contrast to the voices of the mockers surrounding the scene. It may be significant that his rebuke to the second criminal contains an urgent appeal to "fear God" (Luke 23:40). If the man's mockery expresses his extreme lack thereof,[19] the petitioner in his repentance is implicitly shown to tread the path of wisdom, namely, the fear of God.

The paths of criminals and Jesus cross in the hour of humiliation. One mocker's pride is brought down, whereas another humbles himself and is promised exaltation. He is a pivotal piece of the puzzle as one who is last and becomes first, thus embodying the Magnificat's reversal. Yet, the capstone of the scene is Jesus, whose wisdom taught him to suffer "without having done anything amiss" (Luke 23:41). In this way, God's will and glory, the end of wisdom, were served.

---

19. Wisdom literature casts the role of the "mocker" in terms of being in direct antagonism to wisdom and the path of life (cf. Prov 9:12). The opposition is so dogged that mockers are to be left alone (Prov 9:7–8).

5

Reversal and the Lukan *Sondergut* Parables

Reversal of fortune is so paramount to Luke's account that it is fair to say that to speak of his concept of salvation is also to speak of reversal. The concept is rooted in his conviction that all history is salvation history controlled and directed by God alone.[1] Luke's view of history is shaped by the same convictions that informed OT historiography, according to which the sovereign purposes of the God of Israel are enforced among the nations. Although OT historical books record a good deal of fulfillments of divine promises, all of them are provisional and in this sense preparatory of a future act of God's deliverance anticipated in various prophetic oracles. The OT is thus justifiably a testimony conceived in terms of promise. Salvation history comes to a head in Luke-Acts as the author's chronicle of the fulfillment of God's salvific plan both for the remnant of Israel and the Gentile world.[2] Luke therefore is keen on demonstrating God's control of history in drawing attention to how the events of Jesus' birth, ministry, death, and resurrection had been predicted beforehand. In a sweeping utterance from the resurrected Jesus about "all that the prophets have spoken" the sovereign divine will entails the *necessity* of the events surrounding the person of Jesus: "Was it not

---

1. Cf. Emmrich, "The Lucan Account," 267.
2. Sterling, *Historiography*, 359.

necessary (ἔδει) that the Christ should suffer these things and enter into his glory?" (Luke 24:26).³

Perhaps the most definitive expressions of the inviolability of God's sovereign will (βουλή) orchestrating the course of Jesus' life come early on in Luke's second volume, where the claim is stated that Jesus had been "delivered up according to the definite plan and foreknowledge of God" (Acts 2:23), notwithstanding the involvement of "the hands of lawless men" in crucifying the Messiah. Indeed, "both Herod and Pontius Pilate, along with the Gentiles and the people of Israel"⁴ could only "do whatever your [God's] hand and plan had predestined to take place" (Luke 4:28).

In the material unique to Luke's gospel (as well as in Acts⁵) the sovereign eschatological intervention of God is also pronounced, and it is frequently spoken of as the great eschatological reversal.⁶ The world's turning upside down is integral to God's act of deliverance. As we have seen throughout this work, the reversal motif is not only integral to God's salvation plan, but found its way into Israel's wisdom literature. The orientation of wisdom in itself is not particularly eschatological, yet, because it describes God's world order and how one is to respond to it, the same principles inherent in the reversal are also stated in many wisdom texts (cf. Job 33:17; Job 35:12; Ps 10:2; Ps 59:12; Prov 16:18; Prov 18:12; Prov 29:23). The contours of God's involvement in the history of salvation are also discernable elsewhere in creation. The motif of inversion can thus be shown to play a rather consequential role in OT literature overall. Luke saw this important aspect of the divine purpose and work as one of the defining characteristics of the entire sweep of the history of God's salvation (and particularly pertinent to Jesus' teachings) and thus chose to highlight it in the inclusion of material not featured in other gospel records.⁷

3. The account of the Emmaus journey is found nowhere else, although the longer ending of Mark makes a passing remark about the event (Mark 16:12).

4. The inclusion of Herod and Pilate "along with the Gentiles" is likely tailored to correspond with the global language of Ps 2:1–2, where the opposition arrayed against Yahweh's Anointed features the "Gentiles," "the peoples," "the kings of the earth," and "the rulers."

5. Cf. Acts 3:1–10; 9:1–22; 12:6–11, 20–23; 16:16–40; 20:7–12; 22:3–16; 26:12–18, 22–23; 28:23–28.

6. Cf. O'Toole, *The Unity*, 109–48.

7. I would affirm that Luke knew both Mark and Matthew, but even if his knowledge of the latter's work is debatable, the shape of his own record with the inclusion

The fall of Eden brought about a dramatic reversal for humankind (cf. Gen 2:17; Gen 3:16–19), the significance and range of which is already on display in the account of Cain's fratricide, humanity's alienation from God (Gen 3:8–13; Gen 4:1–24), and the abundance of death notices in the genealogies of Genesis 5. However, the first salvific promise of God (Gen 3:15) heralds the defeat of the conqueror and the victory of the conquered. Passing over the patriarchal narratives, which themselves feature an array of reversals pointing to the activity of God, Yahweh's choice of Israel (Deut 7:7) and their subsequent deliverance from their powerful oppressors is the epitome of the OT's two-way reversal, involving salvation for Israel and judgment on their enemies (Exod 15:1–18).

In texts predictive of God's future eschatological intervention on behalf of his elect, salvation is also foretold as the world's turning upside down, and no OT author is more keen on anticipating it than Isaiah, whose writings are supercharged with allusions to a new exodus resulting in a new world order. Isaiah's Apocalypse promises the laying low of the proud (Is 25:11–12) and the humbling of "the inhabitants of the height" (Is 26:5). As for the marginalized people of God, they may look forward to the raising of their dead ones (26:19). The prophetic announcement of the great eschatological exodus and its reversal is particularly overt in Isaiah 35 and embraces virtually all of creation (Is 35:1–7).

That Luke was heavily influenced by the language and the images of Isaiah is no secret. His infancy narrative sets the stage for what follows in the account. The Magnificat casts God's intervention paradigmatically in terms of the reversal of fortunes for the mighty and proud and the lowly on the one hand, the rich and the poor on the other (Luke 1:51–53). Simeon's blessing of Mary and Joseph closes with an unsettling prediction about the child Jesus, as he will effect the "rise and fall" of many in Israel (Luke 2:34). In Luke's account of John the Baptist, he is careful to feature a fuller quotation from Isaiah 40:3–5 against Matthew and Mark, which includes the leveling of the landscape: valleys will be exalted, mountains brought low, and a level highway will be constructed through the undulating wilderness. All this amounts to the salvific program of God (σωτηρία, Luke 3:6), which is a metaphor of the humbling

---

of unique material speaks for itself. The distinguishing factors of Luke's account are quite overt and bespeak his theological agenda whether or not one affirms Matthean priority.

of the proud and the salvation of sinners who repent (or rather, humble themselves).[8]

Again, only Luke chose to include the account of Jesus' inaugural sermon in Nazareth, a scene which rests on a quotation from Isaiah 61:1–2, promising an economic turnabout for the poor (Luke 4:18a, 19) and deliverance for the captives and the oppressed. The blind also will receive sight (Luke 4:18b).[9] Luke therefore shows his familiarity with Isaiah's (or rather, the OT's) concept of the great eschatological reversal already in the opening chapters of his work and points to its fulfillment in the coming of Jesus. Much of the remaining material of the Lukan *Sondergut* expands on this motif, and the Lukan parables form the bulk of the texts unique to the third gospel. A brief survey—barring the parables of Luke 14–16—will show the prominence of the reversal concept in these stories and will conclude our study.

THE GOOD SAMARITAN (LUKE 10:25-37)

The theme of reversal in the Good Samaritan is implicit and correlates with Jesus' challenge to the legal expert. The initial query of the account concerns gaining eternal life (Luke 10:25) in order to close with an examination of "Who is my neighbor?" (Luke 10:29), which is also the main focal point of the popular parable (cf. Luke 10:36). Although the focus shifts, the question of how one is to define the concept of loving one's neighbor is still tied to the lawyer's initial inquiry. It is in the doing of the commandments (loving God and neighbor as oneself, Luke 10:27) that one has life.[10]

The nature of the parable's unsettling challenge posed to the lawyer lies in the problem of identification. The lawyer and other members in

---

8. Cf. Marshall, *The Gospel of Luke*, 137.

9. The Beatitudes (Luke 6:20–24) provide another echo of the statements contained in the Magnificat, insofar as they describe a well-structured two-way reversal, with the rise of the oppressed and the poor balancing the demise of the rich and the esteemed.

10. The question of whether anyone can perfectly fulfill all the demands of the Law is immaterial at this point. Jesus' challenge to the lawyer in pointing him to "what is written in the Law" (Luke 10:26) is coherent on two grounds. First, it meets the expert of the Law on his own turf, forcing him to voice what he knew (but was not doing) all along. Second, the Law *does* promise life on the basis of perfect obedience, irrespective of whether or not one has what it takes to conform to its standards (cf. Lev 18:5; Deut 30:11–15; Ezek 20:11). At any rate, Jesus accepts the lawyer's view that the commandments mark the way to eternal life for the sake of the argument.

his Jewish society "may no longer know where to find themselves in this story."[11] Every story demands some sort of identification on the part of the listener/reader, and the parables certainly insist on the hearer's participation in the communicative process. In the case of the Good Samaritan, the lawyer has to examine himself in relation to all the characters featured in the tale, only to find that he faces nearly impossible choices.

The two clergymen as the presumed heroes of the plot turn out to be a bitter disappointment. They pass by on the other side of the road, leaving the injured man to himself. Should the lawyer identify with these men of elevated social status in the community and admit that, after all, he is like them? Equally impossible would be the option to see himself in the injured man who is a pitiful case study in helplessness. This leaves the man with the unlikely hero of the story, the Samaritan. The shock of seeing the public enemy of the Jews rising above the barriers of a deep-seated and long-standing ethnic and religious feud in order to come to the help of the victim cannot be underestimated.[12] Although the lawyer has to concede that he was "the one who showed mercy" (Luke 10:37), learning what love of neighbor means from an outcast such as the despised Samaritan would have been an unconscionable proposition to any religious Jew. It would have meant to follow a social pariah into a love unburdened of questions of ethnic rifts or religious prejudices. It would have meant becoming an oddball and an outcast oneself. Indeed, the parable's *pointe* casts a long shadow and is capable of shaking to the foundation the barriers erected by any society of humankind at any time, not the least our own.

So, in order to identify with the hero of the story, one has to become what one does not wish to be. In particular, the expert of the Law is called to humble himself and associate with the outcast in fulfilling the love command the way Jesus intended it.[13] He is asked to jettison all his

---

11. Tannehill, *Luke*, 184.

12. For a Jew, the Samaritans were among the least respected people. The mutual hatred between the two ethnic groups is well documented (cf. Josephus, *Ant.* 11.4.9, 114–19; 11.8.6, 341; 12.5.5, 257; Sir. 50:25–26; T. Levi 7:2; Jub. 30:5–6, 23). Many traveling Jews would not even pass through Samaritan territory for fear of defilement. For a detailed discussion see Brindle, "The Origin," 47–75.

13. It is noteworthy that the lawyer's response to Jesus' encouragement to do what he at least in some sense already knew ("Do this, and you will live," Luke 10:28) was to "justify himself" (θέλων δικαιῶσαι ἑαυτὸν, Luke 10:29). Self-justification in Luke is a sign of hubris (cf. Luke 18:9). The most direct indictment against self-justification is found in Luke 16:15. If the lawyer was to take to heart the parable's punch line, his

received convictions and conventions that defined his standing in life and society for the honor of following a Samaritan! The parable is a summons to participate in a reversal by making a radical choice for the unheard-of. It is a call to repentance, a call to humble oneself.

THE RICH FOOL (LUKE 12:13–21)[14]

The wisdom parable makes an important contribution to Luke's theme of wealth and possessions and elucidates the second reversal motif stated in the Magnificat based on economic inversion (Luke 1:53b). Together with the Unjust Steward and the Rich Man and Lazarus, this parable is part of a Lukan triad of stories focusing on the use of money and material resources. Although these parables in and of themselves do not seem to have an eschatological or metaphorical concern and do not require a transfer to some other arena,[15] they are placed in contexts of eschatological import and thus are being informed by their immediate textual environment.[16] In the case of the Rich Fool, the story's frame consisting of instructions about confessing and denying the Son of Man and the final judgment (Luke 12:8–12), as well as Jesus' teachings about anxiety and seeking the kingdom of heaven (Luke 12:22–34) provide an unmistakably eschatological grounding for its message. Consequently, the Rich

---

pride would have to come down.

14. As the context shows (Luke 11:1–4, 11–13), the intricate story of the Friend at Midnight (Luke 11:5–10) is about prayer. It does not contain the reversal motif in its encouragement to approach God with "shamelessness," for which reason it is not featured in this study. However, the word ἀναίδεια describing an overtly negative quality, does deliver a mild shock to the sensitive hearer. All uses of this noun in relevant Greek literature portray a quality that contravenes the established norm (cf. Forbes, *God of Old*, 76). The story promotes a new boldness in approaching the throne of God in prayer. This boldness (or, shamelessness) is not a form of irreverence, but grounded in the character of God revealed in the parable. Inasmuch as this brief story highlights the approachability, familiarity, and closeness of God in terms that would have exploded many conventional conceptions of the Almighty, it invites reflection on (and perhaps correction of) one's picture of God.

15. Crossan argues that the Rich Fool is a metaphor for the kingdom (cf. "Parable and Example," 296). While his conclusion that the story demands a decision informed by the urgency of the kingdom message is sound, the parable itself does not suggest a metaphor of the kingdom. The eschatological concern derives from the parable's placement in its literary context.

16. For the Unjust Steward and the Rich Man and Lazarus see the discussion in chapter 3 of this work.

Fool, along with the two parables of similar concern, requires a fundamental redirection of how one thinks of wealth and possessions in light of discipleship in the kingdom of God.[17] The use of possessions is revelatory of one's true self and one's relation to the kingdom.[18]

The Rich Fool is a negative example of the preposterousness of trusting in possessions, a concept well documented in relevant extra-canonical Jewish writings (cf. Wis. 15:8; Sir 5:1–3, "Do not rely on your wealth, or say, 'I have enough,' for the Lord will surely punish you."; Sir 11:14–20, ". . . I have found rest, and now I shall feast on my goods! . . ."; *1 En.* 97:8–10). His boastful sense of false security finds expression in his soliloquy describing a situation not unlike a leisurely early retirement: "And I will say to my soul, 'Soul, you have many goods laid up for many years; relax, eat, drink, be merry'" (Luke 12:19). Hence, God's verdict "Fool!" is justified. Like the proverbial fool of Ps 14:1 ("The fool says in his heart, 'There is no God.'"), the rich man is one who does not need God and consequently left him out of his calculations for the future.

However, the untimely death of the man and his implicit subsequent judgment[19] shows that God remains to be reckoned with. The fool's failure to lay up treasure for himself toward God and his purposes in life (cf. Luke 12:15, 33) eventually leads to the loss of everything—including life—which spells *total* impoverishment. Once again, the rich has been "sent away empty" (Luke 1:53b), and the dramatic reversal of fortune is complete. Similar to Dives in the Rich Man and Lazarus, the Rich Fool functions as the antipodal image of the manager whose shrewdness led him to make a wise choice with regards to the use of wealth (Luke 16:8–9).

THE BARREN FIG TREE (LUKE 13:6–9)

The preceding material (Luke 13:1–5) furnishes the interpretive key for the parable of the Barren Fig Tree, on account of which no concluding statement of intent such as found in other Lukan parables (cf. Luke 11:9ff.; Luke 12:21; Luke 16:9ff.) is needed. The context describes some

---

17. Snodgrass, *Stories with Intent*, 389.
18. Johnson, *The Literary Function*, 221.
19. Although the parable is primarily about the sudden death of an individual, the judgment is nonetheless implicit, since the reality of its looming after a person's death was a nearly universal religious creed for first century Jews (with the exception of the Sadducees). The notion of accountability to God in the face of the judgment is also pronounced in the preceding pericope (Luke 12:1–12).

people who came to Jesus and told him about two recent disasters in Jerusalem: a massacre of a Galilean party slaughtered by Pilate's troops in the Temple and the collapse of a tower leaving eighteen people dead. Jesus' reaction to this news was to observe that those who had perished in the two events were no worse sinners than other Galileans and residents of Jerusalem. In fact, without repentance, their fate portends the fate of his hearers, a point driven home with additional forte by the verbatim repetition of the ominous phrase, "Unless you repent, you will all likewise perish" (Luke 13:3, 5). It is this warning that reverberates in the parable of the Barren Fig Tree.

Fig trees (and/ or figs) are used in the OT as symbols of the people of Israel (Jer 24:10; Hos 9:10; Mic 7:1). The notion of sitting under one's own vine[20] and fig tree is an important figure of speech pointing to the messianic age (1 Kgs 4:25; Mic 4:4; Zech 3:10).[21] The threatened destruction of the fig tree (and the vine) is predominantly an OT metaphor for judgment on Israel (cf. Jer 29:17; Ezek 17:9; Ezek 19:12–14; Hos 2:12; Joel 1:7, 12; Amos 4:9).[22] In light of this body of OT sub-texts and the parable's immediate literary context, it is difficult to see how this story is not to be read as one specifically about Israel as the people of God.[23] Like John the Baptist's message of repentance, this parable is directed to the entire nation, not merely specific groups within Israel.[24] Accordingly, the warning is against the privileged people of Israel, namely, that the fig tree will be cut down if Israel fails to respond to Jesus' call to repent.[25]

---

20. The mention of the "vineyard" (Luke 13:6) certainly also activates a number of OT texts in which Israel is likened to a vineyard (cf. Ps 80:8–11; Isa 3:14; 5:1–7; 27:2; Jer 2:21). In any case, fig trees and vineyards are associated in several OT texts (Song 2:13; Jer 8:13; Joel 1:7, 12; Mic 4:4). Bailey contends that the parable's OT conceptual motif comes from Isa 5:1–7 and it is therefore targeting the leaders of Judaism (cf. *Through Peasant Eyes* 81–82). On this point, I believe his reading of the parable is too narrow.

21. Similarly, Deut 8:8 describes the promised land as a land of "vineyards and fig trees..."

22. It is to be noted, though, that the metaphor can also refer to judgment on the Gentile nations (Ps 105:33; Isa 34:4).

23. Cf. Snodgrass, *Stories with Intent*, 255ff.

24. There is nothing in this text or its context that warrants the conclusion that a specific group is in view. Indeed, Jesus' inclusive "you all" (Luke 13:3, 5) appears to point in the opposite direction.

25. Wenham, *The Parables of Jesus*, 198.

That repentance (i.e., the fig tree's bearing fruit, Luke 13:7) is more than a reasonable expectation on the part of God is simply assumed in the plot.

Thus, the parable pushes the crisis between God and his people to the brink, only to delay it one more time, offering the hope that judgment will not occur after all. There is a final, yet limited, period of grace, most likely to be identified with Jesus' ministry to Israel.[26] The divine verdict is not final, but if repentance should not materialize, the end of the tree is imminent. The threatened judgment implies a dramatic reversal. The privileged, cared-for people of God who considered their position of being in God's favor as an inviolable creed would be rejected. In this sense, it is also necessary to recall that the parable's demand for repentance (i.e., fruit) walks hand in hand with an implicit call to humility before God. Failure to repent is thus not the result of mere lack of productivity, but indicative of a proud and hardened attitude. While God will exalt "those of humble estate" (Luke 1:52b), the proud will be scattered "in the thoughts of their hearts" (Luke 1:52a).[27]

THE JUDGE AND THE PERSISTENT WIDOW (LUKE 18:1–8)

The parable with its court of law setting is framed by an extended eschatological discourse on the coming Son of Man (Luke 17:20–37) and an additional concluding saying with the same concern for his return (Luke 18:8b). Jesus' interpretive remarks following the story translate the petition of the widow into the vindication of the elect (Luke 18:7). Giving justice to his people may refer to some historical action through which God undertakes for his marginalized people, but in the ultimate sense "vindication" refers to the parousia of the Son of Man as God's final action on behalf of his elect.[28] The said frame of the parable already points in this direction.[29]

---

26. Cf. Nolland, *Luke 9:21—18:34, 719*; Forbes, *God of Old*, 92.

27. Perhaps Jesus' reply to the people who came to him may also betray that, at least as far as they were concerned, they actually *did* think of themselves as "sinners" better than those who met a violent death by default.

28. Cf. Tannehill, *Luke*, 264.

29. The parable corresponds with the disciples' longing predicted in Luke 17:22, namely, to see the days of the victorious Son of Man.

Even though the story promises that God will give justice to his people "soon" (ἐν τάχει, Luke 18:8a),[30] persistence in prayer is part and parcel of its message (cf. Luke 18:1, 7a, "... day and night"). Unlike the judge in his dubious agenda, God shows immediate concern for the petition of his people, according to which he *sets in motion* their vindication, although the final manifestation of it will take time. Hence, persistence is called for. This interpretation highlights the contrast of two conflicting characters: the judge entertained no concern for the widow, not even when he finally took up her case. The character of God, on the other hand, is the very reason why the people of God should never "lose heart" (Luke 18:1), but continue in prayer for vindication, for God will surely make good on his promise.[31]

Inasmuch as the story's eschatological thrust is affirmed, the parable holds out the promised eschatological reversal for the marginalized people of God in the world. The fact that one of the two main characters is a widow is surely significant. In the OT, widows are often portrayed as objects of oppression whose isolated position in society would lead to their being conveniently overlooked or even being targeted for exploitation. God's special care for the lowly and underprivileged is anchored in the Torah (Exod 22:21–24; Deut 10:18; 27:19). The widow is thus a telling representative of the powerless and disadvantaged. In promising them vindication the parable anticipates a dramatic eschatological reversal of fortune in terms stated in the language of the Magnificat (Luke 1:52b, exalting the humble, and, by implication, humbling their oppressors).

---

30. The rendering "soon" is to be preferred over "quickly" in light of the apparent delay of the parousia.

31. In this sense, the difficult phrase, καὶ μακροθυμεῖ ἐπ' αὐτοῖς (Luke 18:7b), is best read as describing God's approachability. While the unjust judge is worn out by the widow's incessant pleading, the same cannot be said about God. He is not put off by the constant petitions presented to him. A similar point (approachability) is made in the parable of the Friend at Midnight (Luke 11:9–13). Cf. Ellis (*The Gospel of Luke*, 213), who renders the phrase, "(will not God vindicate his elect who cry to him day and night) and be patient with them?"

THE PHARISEE AND THE TAX COLLECTOR
(LUKE 18:9-14)

The final Lukan *Sondergut* parable closes with a most familiar punch line: "For everyone who exalts himself will be humbled, but the one who humbles himself will be exalted" (Luke 18:14). The echo of the wisdom saying of Luke 14:11 is unmistakable, and reversal of fortune thus lies at the heart of this passage. That the last of the parables unique to the third gospel closes with an echo of this salient saying indicates its importance for this body of literature and indeed for the work as a whole.

Even though the story is linked to Luke 18:1–8 through the common theme of prayer and the presence of the δικαι-stem (Luke 18:14, δικαιόω), it is also part of a new section stretching all the way through Luke 19:10 focusing on entering the kingdom of God. Insofar as the parable talks about justification, it is here not the parousia which is in view, but forgiveness as a personal experience in time. In the words of Jesus, the parable is about "going home justified" (Luke 18:14).

The two characters represent polar opposites in Jewish society. The Pharisee is respectable and has a certain show of righteousness, nothing of which the tax agent can claim for himself. As a collaborator of Roman imperial power, he was considered a traitor of the Jewish cause and thus ranked among "extortioners, unjust men, and adulterers" (Luke 18:11) at the bottom of the heap. Both of them are quite aware of their apparent situation, and their respective prayers bespeak pride and brokenness, respectively. The tax collector's contrition is illustrated by several remorseful gestures (not lifting his eyes to heaven as a sign of unworthiness, beating his chest as a demonstration of sorrow and grief over his sin, cf. Luke 23:48). His request for propitiation (ἱλάσθητί, Luke 18:13)[32] reveals a deep sense of having offended God and the desire to be forgiven, as well as to enter into a right relationship with him. The desire is granted, and the perfect participle δεδικαιωμένος (Luke 18:14) indicates the divine verdict. The term is forensic, but, as noted above, does not carry the eschatological overtones as in the preceding tale of the widow. It simply describes the man's acceptance before God.

The Pharisee's attitude is almost entirely gathered from his self-referential speech (Luke 18:11–12). Luke's introductory remark (Luke 18:9) prepares the reader for the Pharisee's words. He is utterly convinced of his own righteousness. Not only does he enumerate his religious

---

32. Cf. Marshall, *The Gospel of Luke*, 680; Morris, *Luke*, 265.

performances (Luke 18:12), but his verdict of (self-) righteousness is equally grounded in his contempt for others whom he deems to be more sinful than himself (Luke 18:11). The combination of these two thoughts renders the man incapable of repentance.

The parable intends to highlight the criteria for acceptance with God. Repentance and humility are indispensable characteristics of the person who comes to God. But the story goes further in that it suggests that as long as a sinner humbles himself like the tax agent, the kingdom of heaven knows no restrictions as to who may enter. The doors will open for anyone whatsoever. However, the parable also argues in the opposite direction, maintaining that the doors will remain shut for anyone who fails to humble himself, irrespective of one's social or religious pedigree, something of which the Pharisee believed to have more than enough.[33]

By common Jewish standards, the Pharisee would have been the obvious bet in terms of reception with God. Yet, his rejection shows that God is not at all impressed with rigid tributes and human merit. He wants to see a humble and contrite heart as the fruit of repentance.[34] The tax collector's promotion, on the other hand, was a shock equally difficult to digest. The two characters of the story undergo a dramatic reversal in terms of their *perceived* standing before God and their acceptance of him. Things are not what they seem (cf. Luke 16:15)!

In summary, almost all of the Lukan *Sondergut* parables feature the twin-theme of reversal stated in the Magnificat (Luke 1:51–53) by focusing on one or the other aspect. The wisdom saying of Luke 14:11 (Luke 18:14) epitomizes the reversal motif in almost archetypal terms.[35] While the Magnificat as a song of praise exalts the intervention of God, the saying of Luke 14:11 and the Lukan parables furnish an important qualifier: Human beings do have responsibility to respond to God's initiative in appropriate ways. Failure to do so will bring its own consequences. This raises the question as to how one participates in the reversal.

---

33. The parable has much in common with the story of the Lost Sons (Luke 15:11–32), which, as we saw, was triggered by a Pharisaical complaint over Jesus' association with tax agents and notorious sinners—precisely the kind of people the Pharisee's prayer singles out as pariahs. His self-righteousness also parallels the elder son's rejection of his wayward brother, whereas the younger one's return to his father's house relates well to the tax collector's repentance. Finally, both stories illustrate the compassion of God for the outcast and the castaway.

34. Cf. Herzog, *Subversive Speech*, 173–93.

35. The situation is reminiscent of Jesus' words of rebuke from Luke 16:15, which forms an alternate version of Luke 14:11 and 18:14.

Reversal and the Lukan Sondergut *Parables*

The in-breaking of the kingdom of God is not merely a "love fest," but also an announcement of judgment on the impenitent. Pride which leads to humiliation essentially can have two faces: one is either good enough or rich enough (or possibly both) to bask oneself in a false sense of security. Both attitudes rise to the surface in concentrated form in the controversy depicted in Luke 14–16, but are also found in the remaining Lukan parables scattered throughout the travel narrative. Those who admit their bankruptcy in humble repentance will be received and forgiven, whereas those who think of themselves as just and having no need of repentance (cf. Luke 15:7) become the object of divine judgment. But selfishness and hubris also show in one's attitude towards possessions. Failure to make friends "by means of unrighteous wealth" (Luke 16:9) is fatal and results in the loss of everything. The parables thus issue a call to participate in the subversive work of God by humbling oneself with the promise of exaltation along with the warning against opposition or mere indecision. The call to repentance is universal.

It is crucial to keep in mind that Luke 14–16 (and the rest of the Lukan parables in the travel narrative) lay a most pivotal theological foundation in that the message of reversal of fortune also forms the lens through which the passion narrative wants to be read. The purpose of Jesus' advent was to participate in the eschatological reversal inherent in the message of the kingdom in the most perfect sense. He humbled himself beyond measure in order to be exalted to God's right hand. At the same time, the crucifixion as an act of divine justice serves as an illustration of what the impenitent can expect if they do not pay homage to God's reign in Christ (Acts 17:31).

Conclusion

THE PASSAGE OF LUKE 14–16 forms a highly complex textual unit with its own plot and structure at the heart of the travel narrative and thus Luke's gospel. Its essential function is to furnish a concentrated exposition of the two main themes of reversal from the Magnificat, which not only offer an interpretive key for the three chapters under investigation, but also deliver the author's manifesto for the entire work. The expanded theological blueprint of the Magnificat in Luke 14–16 with its proliferation of material unique to Luke sets the agenda for the gospel in several conspicuous ways.

The high concentration of *Sondergut* parables in this text block is intended to deliver a character profile of the person of God who takes the initiative in Jesus' ministry. The significance of the opening scene relating a Sabbath healing in the house of a ruler of the Pharisees has been discussed in chapter 3 of this work. Jesus' advent inaugurated the sabbatical "year of the Lord's favor" (Luke 4:19). This time of deliverance is marked by a reversal of fortune for the poor and underprivileged, as the quotation from Isa 61:1–2 anticipated, and the restoration of the sick man's health is tangible proof for God's intervention, whose main object is to show mercy, to seek and to save the lost (cf. Luke 19:10).

Nonetheless, God's initiative has a flipside, and both his saving intention as well as the judgment of the impenitent are epitomized in the memorable wisdom saying of Luke 14:11, in which passive voices ("will be humbled," "will be exalted") depict the dualistic nature of the work of God. The following parables and teachings provide a commentary on this principle, revealing both divine mercy and severity. Severity is on display in the parable of the Great Banquet (Luke 14:15–24) in the rejection of the original guests of "honor." Their snubbing of the host's invitation to a lavish dinner occasion is met with a closing comment of ominous finality: "None of those men who were invited shall taste my banquet" (Luke 14:24). In the context of Jesus' ministry, the call to come to the festive occasion translates into God's invitation to enter the kingdom of heaven. Turning one's back on the gracious offer of the gospel is a form of spite which betrays a proud heart, leaving those who decide against the invitation with nothing but the anticipation of a future humiliation in the judgment. They will not be among the blessed "who will eat bread in the kingdom of God" (Luke 14:15).

By the same token, the parable is a stellar portrait of the merciful disposition of the Lord of the eschatological banquet. His expressed desire is that his "house may be filled" (Luke 14:23) with people. While the refusal of the original guests formed the first shock element in the story, the master's order to "bring in the poor and crippled and blind and lame" (Luke 14:21), not to mention the folks of the "highways and hedges" (Luke 14:23), people who were not tolerated in the city, would have seemed equally disturbing to Jesus' listeners. The rich host's home was thus converted into a virtual sick bay and became the festival for the who's who of the community's social pariahs. Not even the story's specific plot, according to which the underprivileged entered the generous man's house only after the insulting response of the first group of invitees, can obscure the fact that God is shown to be no respecter of persons. In fact, his kingdom is for the outcasts who receive exaltation from his gracious hands. God exalts the humble simply because they cannot repay him (cf. Luke 14:14). In this way, the mercy of God is highlighted, mercy, to be sure, that is also extended to the proud who end up spurning the offer.

The nature of God's mercy is particularly overt in the parables of the Lost (Luke 15:1–32), while the aspect of divine severity is completely suspended for the time being. Instead, the language of rejoicing and feasting, a consistent feature throughout Luke 14–16, reaches its climax at this point in the complex.[1] There is "joy in heaven" (Luke 15:7) over

---

1. The theme of banqueting, so prevalent in our three chapters as well as the entire gospel of Luke, also foreshadows how the account of Jesus' life will end, namely in the Passover meal that itself portends Jesus' sacrifice (22:14—23). Indeed, the last Supper forms the theological commentary to the events that follow immediately thereafter and is thus the introduction to the passion narrative. Luke has edited the material in such a way as to make the Passover an integral part of the following account of Jesus' suffering. He achieved this by framing Jesus' final visit to Jerusalem by the repetition of the conspicuous phrase that "they found it just as he had told them" (19:32; 22:13). The reference in 22:13 marks the end of one sub-unit and the beginning of another. Luke's comment of the "hour" having arrived (22:14, a reference to the Passover celebration)

the penitent sinner, and the refrain is to participate in heavenly celebrations, which also forms the challenge Jesus is bringing to the grumbling Pharisees and scribes. God is shown to take the initiative in seeking after the lost in the twin parables of Luke 15:1–10, and the considerable efforts portrayed in the search of both shepherd and woman are reflective of the divine concern invested in what is lost. The joy of having found what was lost depicts the polar opposite of the distress implicit in the initial crisis.

The masterful tale of the Lost Sons highlights the inclusive nature of God's mercy. Not only does the father embrace his homecoming prodigal son with no questions asked, but he also lovingly reaches out to the elder son, whose hardened attitude produces a string of aching insults. The open-ended story puts Jesus' opposition to the test: Will they repent and join the festivities of the coming kingdom? In any case, the parable underscores that God is no respecter of persons. He goes after the outcast as well as the self-righteous.

However, the mercy of God is not extended indefinitely, and the Rich Man and Lazarus moves the growing conflict between Jesus and his adversaries to the bitter conclusion. The function of the rich man as a foil for the agenda of the Pharisees, said to be "lovers of money" (Luke 16:14), is parallel to the role of the elder son in Luke 15. The tale thus points to the inevitable disaster awaiting the impenitent, should they continue in their rejection of the purposes of God. He will humble the proud.

The great reversal portrayed in the parable is the epitome of the Lukan concept of the deliverance of God's people. The reversal is first stated in poetic terms in the Magnificat as a dual transposition of rich and poor, as well as the proud and humble. The wisdom saying of Luke 14:11 forms the general principle of this notion, and Luke 14–16 systematically expounds the reversal maxim along the lines of the twofold emphasis fixed in the Magnificat. In Jesus, God is the initiator of the reversal, but the message of the kingdom also demands participation on the part of the listener. In light of God's plea to be reconciled with him, the response of humbling oneself is indispensable. Failure to do so bespeaks pride which will eventually call for judgment, when the proud will be brought low.

---

opens the account of Jesus' demise and resurrection. Thus, Luke's account ends appropriately with the one meal to which the many earlier scenes of table fellowship have pointed, namely the Passover with the inauguration of the Lord's Supper (22:14—20). The clustering of references to feasting in Luke 14—16 in particular appears to have been designed to point to this Passover celebration with all its theological implications.

Conclusion

The implicit pride of the original invitees of the Great Banquet shows in that they do not judge the host of the occasion, a man of at least equal rank, worthy of their presence. The public insult heaped upon the host sets in motion a story of unprecedented economic reversal, in that the "honorable" are being rejected (Luke 14:24), and the social pariahs are compelled to dine with the rich master of the estate. The resulting scenario describes a world upside down, one that would have been considered absurd by common Greco-Roman societal standards shaped by the *quid pro quo* of patronage and leverage. By associating with the socially disenfranchised the host himself completes the revolution and in this sense humbles himself according to the principle set forth in Luke 14:13–14. The system of reciprocity has been overturned by the call of the kingdom to those who cannot repay the favor.

Yet the parable of the Great Banquet does not leave the reader with any clues as to the psychological landscape of the humble. While the hubris and complacency of the proud is fairly explicit in the lame excuses of Luke 14:18–20, the untouchables are characterized only by their social rank. They cannot be said to have humbled themselves in order to participate in the banquet. The parables of the Lost Sons (Luke 15:11–32) provide the needed psychological profile in affording a case study in repentance, which leads to restoration by a loving father. The repentance of the wayward son illustrates exactly how one is to actively participate in the reversal initiated by God. The son thus humbles himself before the father (after having *been* humbled by destitution) in order to experience the promised exaltation held out in Luke 14:11. As far as the tale goes, his brother persists in self-righteousness, the consequences of which are also predicted in Luke 14:11, notwithstanding an unexpected but possible change of heart.

The parables of the Lost (Luke 15:1–10) form a triad, though, and the first two stories balance the theological message of the final installment. Accordingly, repentance is as much a work involving God as it does the sinner. It is as much a finding of God as it is a being found by him. By frontloading the shorter stories, the reader is reminded of the reality that no one can find the way home without a loving God taking the initiative in seeking the lost.

The twin stories about finding the lost also perform an important function as hermeneutical key to the third parable. Without this prelude, the reader may wonder whether the elder son is to be grouped with his apostate brother or not. But the preceding two stories intimate that "lostness" is not only predicated for one who is far away from home and safety (i.e., the lost sheep, Luke 15:1–7), but one can be lost in a rather domestic setting, too (i.e., the lost coin, Luke 15:8–10). This prepares us to see both sons are lost and in need of repentance. The younger son's condition is rendered in terms of a spatial metaphor. He is a long way from his father's house. Not so with his elder brother, whose alienation from his father is affirmed despite his proximity to him. The parables of the Lost thus underscore the need for both to participate in the reversal, namely the (self-) righteous who needs no repentance (so he may think) and the wayward sinner snared in his own (de)vices.

The theme of reversal continues to inform the texts assembled in Luke 16. The notion may not be quite as obvious in the Unjust Steward (Luke 16:1–9), but the wisdom parable issues yet another call to participate in the reversal by a revolution of the disciple's relationship to possessions, a challenge already posed as early as Luke 14:33, in a passage which also addressed Jesus' followers.[2]

Reversal of fortune forms the backbone of the Rich Man and Lazarus.[3] The two characters' respective transposition fulfills the dictum of the Magnificat's economic inversion (Luke 1:53) as well as the general wisdom principle of Luke 14:11. The rich and the hungry beggar describe the very same contrast suggested in Mary's song of praise, and Abraham's mention of the "good things" (τὰ ἀγαθά, Luke 16:25) provides an additional strong audible link with the Magnificat. The tale is a worthy conclusion to the textual complex of Luke 14–16, since it allows us to see the reversal in its finality, namely, the exaltation of the humble to the heavenly banquet and the humiliation of the rich in Hades.

In banking on the theme of reversal, Luke 14–16 both highlights God's salvific initiative (salvation conceived in terms of reversal of fortune) and issues the call to the listener to actively participate in the revolution of God. The call is to humble oneself by repenting and believing in Jesus. In arranging the text by turns, alternating between those who oppose the call and those who wish to be disciples, Luke can develop the reversal motif "in plain sight" of the two groups of people signified in Luke 14:11.

The eschatological reversal proclaimed in Luke's gospel, however, must be seen in the light of the cross and the resurrection of Jesus. In

---

2. Arguably, the issue already surfaces in Luke 14:12–14 with the call to overturn the codes of reciprocity.

3. The concept is explicitly stated in Luke 16:25.

Conclusion

him, God is both initiator and chief participant in the work of reversal. His being numbered with the outcasts signifies his own voluntary submission to the very principle of reversal taught in Jesus' parables and wisdom instruction.

It bears repetition that the Lukan *Sondergut* parables and in particular the material assembled in Luke 14–16 also preserves a unique memory of Jesus as sage. As we have seen, the Lukan parables are best characterized as wisdom tales. The wise use of money and the virtue and reward of humility are very common traditional wisdom themes in the OT and deutero-canonical literature which intersect with the two reversal motifs in the Magnificat as well as with Luke 14:11. The importance of the sapiential axiom cannot be overstated both for the *Sondergut* and the gospel as a whole. It is surely no accident that the last of the parables unique to Luke's work concludes with a verbatim rehearsal of the wisdom saying in Luke 18:14, thus reiterating the sweeping scope of the reversal initiated by Jesus.

The reversal motif has generally been traced to the prophet Isaiah, certainly with good merit, but, as this study has shown, Luke also has an eye on wisdom, and the salient principle of Luke 14:11 could well be found in OT wisdom literature with its many catchy sayings that bank on reversal in overtly similar ways. Luke's theme of salvation as an eschatological reversal not only harmonizes with much of Israel's wisdom deposits, but also defines the intersection of prophetic and sapiential strands in Luke 14–16. Consequently, all those who humble themselves and participate in the reversal, thereby also choose the wisdom featured in Jesus' instruction. And just as Jesus submitted to his own word by participating in the reversal ordained by God, he is also the embodiment of the wisdom portrayed in Luke 14–16 and elsewhere in the gospel.

Luke's theme of Jesus as sage and storyteller is more pronounced than in the other gospels, and it is an important contribution to the picture drawn of Jesus of Nazareth in the accounts of the NT. The uniqueness of this aspect of Luke's gospel can only be highlighted when we take into consideration that it vanishes from sight in Luke's second volume. Luke therefore was keen on keeping alive the memory of this strand of the complex person of his and our Savior.

Bibliography

Aalen, S. "St. Luke's Gospel and the Last Chapters of Enoch." *New Testament Studies* 13 (1967) 1–13.
Adam, Peter. *Hearing God's Word.* Downers Grove, IL: InterVarsity, 2005.
Allison, Dale. C. *Jesus of Nazareth: Millenarian Prophet.* Minneapolis: Fortress, 1998.
Arens, Edmund. *Kommunikative Handlungen. Die paradigmatische Bedeutung der Gleichnisse Jesu für eine Handlungstheorie.* Düsseldorf: Patmos, 1982.
Arndt, W. F. *The Gospel According to Luke.* St. Louis: Concordia, 1956.
Aus, Roger D. "Luke 15:11–32 and R. Eliezer's Ben Hyrcanus's Rise to Fame." *Journal of Biblical Literature* 104 (1985) 443–69.
———. *Weihnachtsgeschichte—Barmherziger Samariter—Verlorener Sohn: Studien zu ihrem jüdischen Hintergrund.* Berlin: Institut Kirche und Judentum, 1988.
Austin, M. R. "The Hypocritical Son." *Evangelical Quarterly* 57 (1985) 307–15.
Bahr, Heinz E. *Der verlorene Sohn oder die Ungerechtigkeit der Liebe: Das Gleichnis Jesu heute.* Freiburg: Herder, 1993.
Bailey, Kenneth E. *Finding the Lost: Cultural Keys to Luke 15*: St. Louis: Concordia, 1992.
———. "Jacob and the Prodigal: A New Identity Story: A Comparison between the Parable of the Prodigal Son and Gen 27–35." *Theologische Revue* 18 (1997) 54–72.
———. *Jacob and the Prodigal: A Study of the Parable of the Prodigal Son in the Light of the Saga of Jacob.* Downers Grove, IL: InterVarsity, 2003.
———. *Poet and Peasant: A Literary-Cultural Approach to the Parables in Luke.* Grand Rapids: Eerdmans, 1976.
———. *Through Peasant Eyes: More Lucan Parables. Their Culture and Style.* Grand Rapids: Erdmans, 1980.
Ball, Michael. "The Parables of the Unjust Steward and the Rich Man and Lazarus." *Expository Times* 106 (1994–95) 329–30.
———. *The Radical Stories of Jesus. Interpreting the Parables Today.* Oxford: Regents Park College, 2000.
Ballard, Paul. "Reasons for Refusing the Great Supper." *Journal of Theological Studies* 23 (1972) 341–50.
Bauckham, Richard. *The Fate of the Dead.* Leiden: Brill, 1998.
———. "The Rich Man and Lazarus: The Parable and the Parallels." *New Testament Studies* 37 (1991) 225–46.

Bibliography

Baudler, Georg. "Das Gleichnis vom 'betrügerischen Verwalter' (Lk 16:1–13) als Ausdruck der 'inneren Biographie' Jesu." *Theologie der Gegenwart* 28 (1985) 65–76.

———. *Jesus im Spiegel seiner Gleichnisse*. Stuttgart: Calver, 1986.

Beale, G. K., and D. A. Carson, editors. *Commentary on the New Testament Use of the Old Testament*. Grand Rapids: Baker, 2007.

Bindemann, Walter. "Ungerechte Vorbilder? Gottesreich und Gottesrecht in den Gleichnissen Vom 'ungerechten Verwalter' und 'ungerechten Richter.'" *Theologische Literaturzeitung* 120 (1995) 955–70.

Bloomberg, Craig L. *Contagious Holiness—Jesus' Meals with Sinners*. Downers Grove, IL: InterVarsity, 2005.

———. *Interpreting the Parables*. Downers Grove, IL: InterVarsity, 1990.

———. "Interpreting the Parables of Jesus: Where Are We and Where Do We Go from Here?" *Catholic Biblical Quarterly* 53 (1991) 50–78.

———. *The Historical Reliability of the Gospels*. Downers Grove, IL: InterVarsity, 1987.

Bock, Darrell L. *Luke 1:1—9:50*. Grand Rapids: Baker, 1994.

———. *Luke 9:51—24:53*. Grand Rapids: Baker, 1996.

Bosch, Dietrich. *Die Heidenmission in der Zukunftsschau Jesu. Eine Untersuchung zur Eschatologie der synoptischen Evangelien*. Zürich: Zwingli, 1959.

Bosley, Harold A. *He Spoke to Them in Parables*. New York: Harper, 1963.

Bovon, François. *Das Evangelium nach Lukas*. 3 Bände: Zürich: Benziger, 1989–2001.

———. *Luke the Theologian: Fifty-Five Years of Research (1950–2005)*. Waco: Baylor University Press, 2006.

Bowen, C. Edward. "The Parable of the Unjust Steward: Oikos as the Interpretive Key." *Expository Times* 112 (2001) 314–15.

Braun, Willi. *Feasting and Social Rhetoric in Luke 14*. Cambridge: Cambridge University Press, 1995.

Brindle, W. A. "The Origin and History of the Samaritans." *Grace Theological Journal* 5 (1984) 47–75.

Broer, I. "Das Gleichnis vom verlorenen Sohn und die Theologie des Lukas." *New Testament Studies* 20 (1973) 453–62.

Brown, Colin. "The Parable of the Rebellious Son." *Scottish Journal of Theology* 51 (1998) 391–405.

Bryan, Steven M. *Jesus and Israel's Traditions of Judgment and Restoration*. Cambridge: Cambridge University Press, 2002.

Carey, W. Gregory. "Excuses, Excuses: The Parable of the Banquet (Luke 14:15–24) within the Larger Context of Luke." *Irish Biblical Studies* 17 (1995) 177–87.

Cassidy, Robert J. *Jesus, Politics, and Society: A Study of Luke's Gospel*. New York: Orbis, 1978.

Charnock, S. *The Existence and Attributes of God*, Vol. I. Grand Rapids: Baker, 1979.

Combrink, Hans, J. B. "A Social-Scientific Perspective on the Parable of the Unjust Steward." *Neotestamentica* 30 (1996) 281–306.

Crossan, John D. *Cliffs of Fall: Paradox and Polyvalence in the Parables of Jesus*. New York: Seabury, 1980.

———. "Parable and Example in the Teaching of Jesus." *New Testament Studies* 18 (1971–72) 285–307.

Culpepper, Robert A. *The New Interpreter's Bible*, Vol. IX, *Luke–John*. Nashville: Abingdon, 1995.

Bibliography

Curkpatrick, Stephen. "A Parable Frame-up and Its Audacious Reframing." *New Testament Studies* 48 (2003) 22–38.

———. "Dissonance in Luke 18:1–8." *Journal of Biblical Literature* 121 (2002) 107–21.

———. "Parable Metonymy and Luke's Kerygmatic Framing." *Journal for the Study of the New Testament* 25 (2003) 289–307.

Danker, Frederick W. *Jesus and the New Age: A Commentary on St. Luke's Gospel.* Philadelphia: Fortress, 1985.

Dempster, Steve G. *Dominion and Dynasty.* Downers Grove, IL: InterVarsity, 2003.

Derret, J. Duncan M. *Law in the New Testament.* London: Darton, Longman & Todd, 1970.

———. "The Parable of the Two Sons." *Studia Theologica* 25 (1971) 109–16.

Dodd, C. H. *The Parables of the Kingdom.* London: Nisbet, 1936.

Donahue, J. *The Gospel in Parable.* Philadelphia: Fortress, 1988.

Drury, John. *The Parables in the Gospels.* New York: Crossroad, 1985.

Dupont, J. "Le Magnificat comme Discours sur Dieu." *La nouvelle revue theologique* 102 (1980) 321–43.

Eckey, Wilfried. *Das Lukasevangelium.* Teilband II, *11:1—24:53.* Neukirchen-Vluyn: Neukirchener, 2004.

Egelkraut, Hans L. *Jesus' Mission to Jerusalem: A Redaction Critical Study of the Travel Narrative in the Gospel of Luke, 9:51—19:44.* Frankfurt/Main: Lang, 1976.

Ellis, E. Earle. *The Gospel of Luke.* Grand Rapids: Eerdmans, 1996.

Emmrich, Martin. "The Lukan Account of the Beelzebul Controversy." *Westminster Theological Journal* 62 (2000) 267–79.

Esler, Phillip F. *Community and Gospel in Luke–Acts: The Social and Political Motivations of Lucan Theology.* Cambridge: Cambridge University Press, 1987.

Evans, C. A. "Parables in Early Judaism." In *The Challenge of Jesus' Parables*, edited by R. N. Longenecker, 51–78. Grand Rapids: Eerdmans, 2000.

Evans, C. A., and J. Sanders, editors. *Luke and Scripture.* Minneapolis: Fortress, 1993.

Farmer, W. R. *The Synoptic Problem: A Critical Analysis.* Macon: Mercer University Press, 1964.

Fiebig, Peter. *Die Gleichnisreden Jesu im Lichte der rabbinischen Gleichnisse des Neutestamentlichen Zeitalters.* Tübingen: Mohr-Siebeck, 1912.

Fields, L. M. "Proverbs 11:30: Soul-Winning or Wise Living?" *Journal of the Evangelical Theologial Society* 50 (2007) 517–35.

Fisher, Neal. *The Parables of Jesus.* New York: Crossroad, 1990.

Fitzmeyer, Joseph A. *The Gospel According to Luke X–XXIV.* Garden City: Doubleday, 1985.

Fletcher, Donald R. "The Riddle of the Unjust Steward: Is Irony the Key?" *Journal of Biblical Literature* 82 (1963) 15–30.

Forbes, Greg W. *The God of Old: The Role of the Lukan Parables in the Purpose of Luke's Gospel.* Sheffield: Sheffield Academic, 2000.

Ford, Richard Q. *The Parables of Jesus: Recovering the Art of Listening.* Minneapolis: Fortress, 1997.

France, R. T., and D. Wenham, editors. *Gospel Perspectives I.* Sheffield: JSOT, 1980.

Funk, Robert W. *Parables and Presence.* Philadelphia: Fortress, 1982.

Geldenhuys, N. *Commentary on the Gospel of Luke.* Grand Rapids: Zondervan, 1951.

Gerhardsson, B. "If We Do Not Cut the Parables out of Their Frames." *New Testament Studies* 37 (1991) 321–35.

Bibliography

Gnilka, Joachim. *Jesus of Nazareth: Message and History*. Peabody: Hendrickson, 1997.

Gooding, David. *According to Luke. A New Exposition of the Third Gospel*. Leicester: InterVarsity, 1987.

Goulder, Michael D. *Luke: A New Paradigm*. 2 vols. Sheffield: JSOT, 1989.

Gowler, David B. *Host, Guest, Enemy and Friend: Portraits of the Pharisees in Luke and Acts*. New York: P. Lang, 1991.

———. *What Are They Saying about the Parables?* Mahwah: Paulist, 2000.

Gray, P., and G. O'Day, editors. *Scripture and Traditions: Festschrift for Carl R. Holladay*. Leiden: Brill, 2008.

Green, Joel B. *The Gospel of Luke*. Grand Rapids: Eerdmans, 1997.

Greene, M. Dwaine. "The Parable of the Unjust Steward as Question and Challenge." *Expository Times* 112 (2000) 82–87.

Grundmann, Walter. *Das Evangelium nach Lukas*. Berlin: Evangelische Verlagsanstalt, 1963.

Hendrickx, Herman. *The Parables of Jesus*. San Francisco: Harper & Row, 1986.

Herzog, William R. *Jesus, Justice, and the Reign of God: A Ministry of Liberation*. Louisville: Westminster, 2000.

———. *Parables as Subversive Speech. Jesus as the Pedagogue of the Oppressed*. Louisville: Westminster, 1994.

Hintzen, Jochen. *Verkündigung un Wahrnehmung: Über das Verhältnis von Evangelium und der Leser an Beispiel Lk 16,19–31 im Rahmen des lukanischen Doppelwerkes*. Frankfurt/Main: Hain, 1991.

Hock, Ronald F. "Lazarus and Micyllus: Greco-Roman Backgrounds to Luke 16:19–31." *Journal of Biblical Literature* 106 (1987) 447–63.

Hofius, Otfried. "Alttestamentliche Motive im Gleichnis vom verlorenen Sohn." *New Testament Studies* 24 (1977) 240–48.

Hoppe, R. "Gleichnis und Situation: Zu den Gleichnissen vom guten Vater (Lk 15:11–32) und Gütigen Hausherrn (Matt 20:1–5)." *Biblische Zeitschrift* 28 (1984) 1–21.

Hultgren, Arland J. *The Parables of Jesus. A Commentary*. Grand Rapids: Eerdmans, 2000.

Hunter, A. M. *Interpreting the Parables*. London: SCM, 1960.

Ireland, Dennis J. *Stewardship and the Kingdom of God: An Historical, Exegetical, and Contextual Study of the Parable of the Unjust Steward*. Leiden: Brill, 1993.

Jeremias, Joachim *The Parables of Jesus*. London: SCM, 1963.

———. "Tradition und Redaktion in Lukas 15." *Zeitschrift für die neutestamentliche Wissenschaft und die Kunde der älteren Kirche* 62 (1971) 172–89.

Johnson, Luke T. *The Gospel of Luke*. Collegeville: Liturgical, 1991.

———. *The Literary Function of Possessions in Luke–Acts*. Missoula: Scholars, 1977.

Jones, Peter R. *Studying the Parables of Jesus*. Macon: Smyth & Helwys, 1999.

Jülicher, Adolf. *Die Gleichnisreden Jesu*. Darmstadt: Wissenschaftliche Buchgesellschaft, 1963.

Just, Arthur J. *Luke 9:51—24:53*. St. Louis: Concordia, 1997.

Kidner, D. *The Wisdom of Proverbs, Job and Ecclesiastes*. Downers Grove, IL: InterVarsity, 1985.

Kilgallen, John J. *A Brief Commentary on the Gospel of Luke*. Mahwah: Paulist, 1988.

———. "Luke 15 and 16: A Connection." *Biblica* 78 (1997) 369–76.

———. "The Purpose of Luke's Divorce Text (16,18)." *Biblica* 76 (1995) 229–38.

Bibliography

Kissinger, W. S. *The Parables of Jesus: A History of Interpretation and Bibliography.* New Jersey: Scarecrow, 1979.
Kistemaker, Simon J. *The Parables of Jesus.* Grand Rapids: Baker, 1980.
Kloppenborg, John. "The Dishonoured Master (Luke 16:1–8a)." *Biblica* 70 (1989) 134–59.
Klostermann, Erich. *Das Lukasevangelium.* 3rd ed. Handbuch zum Neuen Testament 5. Tübingen: Mohr Siebeck, 1975.
Landmesser, Christof. "Die Rückkehr ins Leben nach dem Gleichnis vom verlorenen Sohn (Lukas 15:11–32)." *Zeitschrift für Theologie und Kirche* 99 (2002) 239–61.
Landry, David, and Ben May. "Honor Restored: New Light on the Parable of the Prudent Steward (Luke 16:1–8a)." *Journal of Biblical Literature* 119 (2000) 287–309.
Laniak, Tim S. *Shepherds after My Own Heart—Pastoral Traditions and Leadership in the Bible.* Downers Grove, IL: InterVarsity, 2006.
Lehtipuu, O. *The Afterlife Imagery in Luke's Story of the Rich Man and Lazarus.* Leiden: Brill, 2007.
Longenecker, Richard N., editor. *The Challenge of Jesus' Parables.* Grand Rapids: Eerdmans, 2000.
Marshall, I. Howard. *Eschatology and the Parables.* London: Tyndale, 1963.
———. *The Gospel of Luke.* Grand Rapids: Eerdmans, 1978.
Mathewson, Dave L. "The Parable of the Unjust Steward (Luke 16:1–13): A Reexamination of the Traditional View in Light of Recent Challenges." *Journal of the Evangelical Theologial Society* 38 (1995) 29–39.
McArthur, Harvey K., and Robert M. Johnston. *They Also Taught in Parables.* Grand Rapids: Eerdmans, 1990.
McKnight, Scot. *Interpreting the Synoptic Gospels.* Grand Rapids: Baker, 1988.
Menzies, Robert. "The Lost Coin." *Expository Times* 64 (1953) 274–76.
Metzger, Bruce. *A Textual Commentary on the Greek New Testament.* London: UBS, 1971.
Milne, Douglas J. W. "The Father with Two Sons: A Modern Reading of Luke 15." *Themelios* 27 (2001) 12–21.
Morris, Leon. *Luke.* Grand Rapids: Eerdmans, 2002.
Morschauser, Scott. "Revolutionary Economics? Once Again, the Parable of the Steward." *JHC* 8 (2001) 49–67.
Neyrey, J. H., editor. *The Social World of Luke–Acts: Models for Interpretation.* Peabody: Hendrickson, 1991.
Nolland, John. *Luke 9:21—18:34.* Dallas: Word Books, 1993.
O'Toole, Robert F. *The Unity of Luke's Theology: An Analysis of Luke–Acts.* Wilmington: Glazier, 1984.
Palmer, Harold. "Just Married, Cannot Come." *Novum Testamentum* 18 (1976) 241–57.
Parsons, Mikael C. "Landmarks along the Way: The Function of the 'L' Parables in the Lukan Travel Narrative." *Southwestern Journal of Theology* 40 (1997) 33–47.
Petzhold, Martin. *Gleichnisse Jesu und christlich Dogmatik.* Göttingen: Vandenhoeck & Ruprecht, 1984.
Petzke, Gerd. *Das Sondergut des Evangeliums nach Lukas.* Zürich: Theologischer, 1990.
Piper, John. *The Pleasures of God: Meditations on God's Delight in Being God.* Sisters: Multnomah, 2000.

Bibliography

Pöhlmann, Wolfgang. *Der verlorene Sohn und das Haus. Studien zu Lukas 15:11–32 im Horizont der antiken Lehre vom Haus, Erziehung und Ackerbau*. Tübingen: Mohr-Siebeck, 1993.

Pokorny, Petr. *Theologie der lukanischen Schriften*. Göttingen: Vandenhoeck & Ruprecht, 1998.

Preisker, Hans. "Lukas 16,1–7." *Theologische Literaturzeitung* 74 (1949) 85–92.

Ratzinger, Joseph. *Jesus of Nazareth*. New York: Doubleday, 2007.

Rengstorf, Karl H. *Die Re-Investitur des verlorenen Sohnes in der Gleichniserzählung Jesu, Luk. 15:11–32*. Köln: Westdeutscher, 1967.

Resseguie, John L. "Interpretation of Luke's Central Section (Luke 9:51—19:44) since 1856." *SBTh* 5 (1975) 3–36.

Ringe, Sharon H. *Luke*. Louisville: Westminster, 1995.

Ringgren, Helmer. "Luke's Use of the Old Testament." *Harvard Theological Review* 79 (1986) 227–35.

Sanders, E. P. *Judaism: Practice and Belief 63 BCE–66 CE*. London: SCM, 1992.

Schottroff, L. "Das Gleichnis vom verlorenen Sohn." *Zeitschrift für Theologie und Kirche* 68 (1971) 27–52.

Shellard, Barbara. *New Light on Luke. Its Purpose, Sources, and Literary Context*. Sheffield: Sheffield Academic, 2002.

Shillington, V. George, editor. *Jesus and His Parables*. Edinburgh: T. & T. Clark, 1997.

Sider, John. *Interpreting the Parables: A Hermeneutical Guide to Their Meaning*. Grand Rapids: Zondervan, 1995.

Singer, Christophe. "La difficulté d'être disciple: Luc 14/25–35." *Etudes théologiques et religieuses* (1998) 21–36.

Sloan, Robert B. *The Favorable Year of the Lord: A Study of Jubilary Theology in the Gospel of Luke*. Austin: Schola, 1977.

Smith, C. W. F. *The Jesus of the Parables*. Philadelphia: United Church Press, 1975.

Snider, John W. "Rediscovering the Parables: The Logic of the Jeremias Tradition." *Journal of Biblical Literature* 102 (1983) 61–83.

Snodgrass, Klyne. "From Allegorizing to Allegorizing: A History of the Interpretation of the Parables." In *The Challenge of Jesus' Parables*, edited by R. N. Longenecker, 3–29. Grand Rapids: Eerdmans, 2000.

———. "A Hermeneutics of Hearing Informed by the Parables with Special Reference to Mark 4." *Bulletin for Biblical Research* 14 (2004) 59–79.

———. *Stories with Intent. A Comprehensive Guide to the Parables of Jesus*. Grand Rapids, Eerdmans, 2008.

Stagg, Frank. "Luke's Theological Use of Parables." *Review and Expositor* 94 (1997) 215–31.

———. *Studies in Luke's Gospel*. Nashville: Convention, 1965.

Steele, E. S. "Luke 11:37–54—A Modified Hellenistic Symposium?" *Journal of Biblical Literature* 103 (1984) 379–94.

Stein, Robert H. *Luke*. Nashville: Broadman, 1992.

———. *The Synoptic Problem: An Introduction*. Grand Rapids: Baker, 1987.

Sterling, G. E. *Historiography and Self-Definition*. Leiden: Brill, 1992.

Strack, H. L., and P. Billerbeck. *Kommentar zum Neuen Testament aus Talmud und Midrasch*, Band II. München: C. H. Beck, 1956.

Talbert, Charles H. *Reading Luke—A Literary and Theological Commentary on the Third Gospel*. Macon, GA: Smyth & Helwys, 2002.

Tannehill, Robert C. *Luke*. Nashville: Abingdon, 1996.

———. "The Magnificat as Poem." *Journal of Biblical Literature* 93 (1974) 263-75.

———. *The Narrative Unity of Luke-Acts: A Literary Interpretation*, vol. 1: *The Gospel According to Luke*. Philadelphia: Fortress, 1986.

Thielicke, Helmut. *The Waiting Father*. New York: Harper & Row, 1959.

Thiselton, Anthony C. "Reader Responsibility Hermeneutics." In *The Responsibility of Hermeneutics*, by Roger Lundin, Clarence Walhout, and Anthony C. Thiselton, 79-114. Grand Rapids: Eerdmans, 1985.

The Responsibility of Hermeneutics. Grand Rapids: Eerdmans, 1985.

Tolbert, M. A. *Perspectives on the Parables*. Philadelphia: Fortress, 1979.

———. "The Prodigal Son: An Essay in Literary Criticism from a Psychoanalytical Perspective." *Semeia* 9 (1977) 1-20.

Van Der Los, H. *The Miracles of Jesus*. Leiden: Brill, 1965.

Weiss, Bernd. *Die Evangelien des Markus und Lukas*. Göttingen: Meyer, 1901.

Wendland, Ernst R. "Finding Some Lost Aspects of Meaning in Christ's Parables of the Lost—And Found (Luke 15)." *Trinity Journal* 17 (1996) 19-65.

Wenham, David. *The Parables of Jesus*. Downers Grove, InterVarsity, 1989.

Witherington, Ben III. *Jesus the Sage. The Pilgrimage of Wisdom*. Minneapolis: Fortress, 2000.

Wittig, Susan. "A Theology of Multiple Meanings." *Semeia* 9 (1977) 75-103.

Wolter, Michael. "Lk 15 Als Streitgespräch." *Ephemerides theologicae lovanienses* 78 (2002) 25-56.

Young, Brad H. *Jesus and His Jewish Parables: Rediscovering the Roots of Jesus' Teaching*. New York: Paulist, 1989.

———. *The Parables. Jewish Tradition and Christian Interpretation*. Peabody: Hendrickson, 1998.

www.ingramcontent.com/pod-product-compliance
Lightning Source LLC
Chambersburg PA
CBHW070915160426
43193CB00011B/1475